FIGHTING SEXUAL HARASSMENT

WRITTEN AND COORDINATED BY
Connie Backhouse, Rags Brophy, Alice Friedman,
Martha Hooven, Beth Johnson, Freada Klein,
Margaret Lazarus, Anne Lopes, Lynn Rubinett,
Kate Swann, Denise Wells

EDITOR
Wendy Sanford

GRAPHICS
Vicki Gabriner

SPECIAL THANKS TO
Boston Women's Healthbook Collective

FIGHTING SEXUAL HARASSMENT

AN ADVOCACY HANDBOOK

copublished by
Alyson Publications, Inc.
and
The Alliance Against Sexual Coercion
Boston, Massachusetts

Table of Contents

Chapter One

The Purpose of This Book

In June of 1976, the Alliance Against Sexual Coercion was formed to work against sexual harassment in the workplace. Sexual harassment emerged as a separate public issue out of the anti-rape movement: the three Boston women who founded AASC had previously been involved in rape crisis center work. The unique problems encountered by women who had been sexually abused by their bosses or co-workers demonstrated the need for a strategy to fight the many forms of workplace sexual harassment, which included not only rape, but all the kinds of sexual pressure that women experience in their working lives.

Since June of 1977, AASC has offered direct services to women workers. These include emotional support, unemployment compensation information for women who quit their jobs because of harassment, legal options and referrals, vocational and educational counseling referrals, and rap groups. To provide the kind of services women wanted we have researched the problem and contacted rape crisis centers and working women's organizations across the country. Most importantly, our services grow out of the expressed wants and needs of the women who contact us.

AASC's experience in providing outreach and direct services leads us to believe that the most effective means of dealing with sexual harassment is to incorporate sexual harassment services into existing agencies, community centers and working women's groups. If appropriate training and information are made available for social service workers, community mental health workers, job counselors, union personnel, and women's groups, a large number of working women can be served.

Clients of social service agencies are often experiencing sexual harassment at their workplace, but frequently the sexual harassment elements go undetected by the agencies and often even by the women themselves. (See Chapter 5 and 8.) Since most women feel very alone in the situation and usually don't talk freely about being sexually harassed, it takes special efforts on the part of agency workers and other advocates to recognize this particular problem.

It is critical that social service agencies learn to identify when their clients are being sexually harassed. Not to do so can cause misdirected counseling which fails to deal with the real source of the problem. If community agencies and work advocates are aware of sexual harassment as a serious problem, many more women will feel freer to talk about the issue where they normally go for help and services. The sensitizing of existing organizations will allow for greater outreach, contact, and help for those who need it. *The purpose of this book is to train people in all kinds of social service work to recognize when women seeking their assistance are experiencing sexual harassment, and to provide some guidelines on how to deal with this problem.*

AASC will continue to provide information and training sessions for any interested organization. We will also continue to raise the issue and keep it in the public's awareness, to distribute materials containing practical strategies for working women on dealing with sexual harassment, to provide workplace and community educational programs, and to investigate legal and direct action alternatives. We plan to continue as long as possible to act as a resource group for any agencies or groups providing sexual harassment services to their clients.

Chapter Two
Definition of Sexual Harassment

Sexual harassment is any unwanted sexual attention a woman experiences on the job, ranging from leering, pinching, patting, verbal comments, and subtle pressure for sexual activity, to attempted rape and rape. The sexual harasser may be the woman's employer, supervisor, co-worker, client, or customer. In addition to the anxiety caused by sexual demands made by bosses, there is the implicit message from the harasser that non-compliance will lead to reprisals. These reprisals can include escalation of the harassment, poor work assignments, sabotaging of a woman's work, sarcasm, unsatisfactory job evaluations, threatened demotions, transfers, denial of raises and benefits and promotions, and, in the final analysis, dismissal and a poor job reference. In a society where jobs are scarce and racial and ethnic inequalities persist, the coercive nature of workplace sexual harassment intensifies, particularly for Third World women.* For economic and/or emotional reasons, no woman can afford to lose her job. Sexual harassment deepens the economic vulnerability women workers experience.

A number of examples may serve to illustrate the problem of sexual harassment more clearly.

Case Study #1

Carol is the administrative director of a community health center. She is black and has been employed for three years. She has performed her job well, acquired a diversity of skills, and been promised opportunities for advancement to an executive director. Her boss, the director of her division, is also well-respected; he is a middle-aged white man, married for nearly 20 years and the father of three children. Over the past few months he has extended dinner invitations to her several times as a way to "get to know each other better." Buying her flowers and small presents has also become a recent habit. Carol has politely but firmly refused the dinner invitations; similarly, she has thanked him for the gifts while expressing that receiving them makes her feel uncomfortable. The division director expressed surprise at her response and indicated that she had given indications of interest in him. When she questioned him, it turned out that he expected her to be more relaxed about sex because of her racial background. As soon as the company offered a new training program for administrators. Carol applied; she viewed this as a way not only to advance her own goals, but as a way out of the chronic tension she endured at work. Her application was denied. After a long and frustrating search for an explanation, Carol was told by Personnel that her boss had evaluated her as "uncooperative" and stated that the "quality of her work had steadily declined." She now feels trapped in a dead-end job — the victim of sexual and racial harassment undergoing constant stress as a result of her boss's advances.

Case Study #2

Sandy is a 38-year-old white divorcee with teenage children. She works as the only woman electrician on a construction site. While she has not yet experienced sexual harassment from her boss, she is subjected to a great deal of harassment from her male mainly white co-workers. When she began working on the site, her co-workers would hoot, holler, whistle and stamp their feet every time she walked by them. When it became clear that these tactics were not enough to make Sandy quit, their behavior escalated. Several of them began to get physical with her, grabbing her and pinching her. She began to receive obscene phone calls and threatening letters at home. One of her fellow-workers went so far as to put a dildo in her lunch bucket. Although Sandy feels alienated and lonely, she wants to try and stay in the job, hoping her co-workers will eventually accept her as an equal.

---

*We use the term "Third World" to mean Black, Hispanic, Chicana, Latina, Native American and other people of color who have been subjected to discrimination/oppression based on their racial identities.

Case Study #3

Rosalie is a 23-year-old waitress, single, white and without children. She worked for some years as a cocktail waitress at a fancy hotel and recently began to interview for jobs as a waitress in expensive restaurants. At her second job interview, the manager, a young white man, began touching her while discussing her waitressing experience. She tried to get him to stop but he continued and started to rip off her blouse. She hit him and was able to get away. Of course she didn't get the job.

All of these case studies are instances of sexual harassment, which is a subtle but serious form of violence against women. All women are targets for this kind of male behavior in normal social settings and to some extent on the streets. On the work scene, however, women's vulnerability increases dramatically. Sexual harassment becomes coercive in this context because it is supported by and can be enforced through the use of economic power. To refuse sexual demands from those who control one's livelihood is to endanger that livelihood. Given women's position in the workplace — low wages, low status occupations and high unemployment — the possibility for sexual coercion escalates.

The issues raised by most sexual harassment are significantly different from those evoked by rape. For example, women who experience harassment are often trapped in abusive situations due to the scarcity of jobs and the level of skill and training available to women in this society. If a woman chooses to remain at her workplace, she must be prepared to be confronted by her harasser on an on-going basis. She must also cope with the anxiety of trying to do a good job despite her boss's power to demote, fire or give her a poor performance review because she will not comply with his demands. This creates a special situation of stress for the woman worker.

When a woman is harassed at the workplace, her response is one of both anxiety and fear. Questions come to her mind: Will she be able to continue working under these conditions? Did she provoke the situation? Will her boss ever stop? What is the best way to deal with him? Is there any predictability to his behavior? How can she both cope with the fear of losing her job if she does not comply, and cope with the anxiety provoked by the insistence of his demands? According to studies done on occupational health and safety, the economic insecurity she experiences because she can be fired for not consenting to her boss' demands, is in itself, a major cause of workplace stress. When this is added to a fear of sexual assault, the stress level rises intolerably.

Why Men Harass

The reasons why men harass are complex. The society we live in is characterized by economic instability, an ever-tightening job market, and few opportunities for people to exercise control over their lives. Women have become a significant part of the workforce — they now compete for jobs that are traditionally male preserves (carpentry and business administration, for example). Men may feel that they can't measure up to the standard inherent in the traditional male role. They have little control over this situation, and yet the role of provider is an important source of identity for most men. The ensuing conflict must be resolved by each individual — one form this takes is sexual harassment of women workers who are *de facto* less powerful than males. Sexual harassment is *not* an expression of sexual frustration or desire.

We have found men in all types of jobs — the top levels of government, professions, and others — harass women at work. (So it's not just a matter of feeling powerless at work.) Regardless of their position in society, all men have a choice whether or not to engage in sexual harassment. Some men choose to assert power over women in this way. Thus the power relationship inherent in our culture, and our culture's scorn for women, is maintained in the individual's experience.

A further complicating factor is assessing why men harass women is that many men have difficulty in distinguishing between coercive and consensual relationships — i.e., sexual harassment and the office romance. This confusion is not limited to the workplace, but exists whenever and wherever men and women interact.

The Relationship Between the Sexual Revolution and Sexual Harassment

Sexual attitudes and practices have changed dramatically over the last several years. To some extent these changes have been made possible through the development of more effective — though not necessarily safer — forms of birth control. Heterosexual relations are occurring at a younger age, and both premarital and extramarital sexual activity are reported more frequently now than in earlier years. The effects of the so-called "sexual revolution" on the incidence of sexual harassment at the workplace are complex.

The sexual revolution is often confused with the women's liberation movement. What the sexual revolution and the women's movement had in common was the questioning of existing definitions of male and female sexuality, and the understanding of sexuality as a form of human communication rather than for procreation alone. However, the women's movement has questioned not just sexual relationships but *all* power relationships between men and women in society, as well as the whole cultural context in which sexuality is expressed. It is arguable that the sexual revolution was harmful to women because it did not challenge basic social structures. Women are still taught to evaluate our worth in terms of our sexual and reproductive capacities. We are expected to make the best bargain possible on a marriage market, exchanging these assets for future financial and emotional security. Since we as women are still in the position of having to barter with our sexuality, it is not surprising that men attempt to persuade and coerce us into granting sexual favors, trying to get the best deal they can. Their actions range from the promise of economic reward through the economic coercion of sexual harassment to physical force such as rape.

In other words, the sexual revolution may have only exchanged a new sexual mythology and set of pressures for the old ones. Previously, men were viewed as having strong sex drives, while most women were portrayed as not interested in sexual activity — sex was a duty, not a mutually pleasurable experience. This difference in sex drives was often used as the justification/explanation of rape and violence against women. Recently, women are defining ourselves as sexual beings. While this may have made it easier for women to assert our needs, it also made it more difficult for women to say no to men. Even though more flexibility in defining sex roles for both men and women was gained, women found ourselves in a new double-bind. If a "liberated" woman said no, she was stigmatized as strange, with the additional labels of traditional, repressed and difficult. This new social acceptance of sexuality, while clearly important and necessary, gives men as well as women, a whole new set of difficulties which can be expressed in the form of workplace sexual harassment. For example, since women are viewed as interested in sex, men might feel that the new openness around sexuality gives them an opportunity to make sexual overtures while ignoring other kinds of power they hold which interfere with a woman's ability to say yes or no.

Women's current striving for independence, including sexual independence, has been blamed as the "cause" of increased violence against women. We as women are still held responsible. By questioning the relationships between men and women, and women's status in society, women are not asking to be violated. The fact that sexual harassment took place before the sexual revolution, and hasn't stopped since the sexual revolution, indicates that sexual harassment is not about sexuality alone. In sexual harassment, gender and sexuality are being used as the basis for establishing power differentials in society.

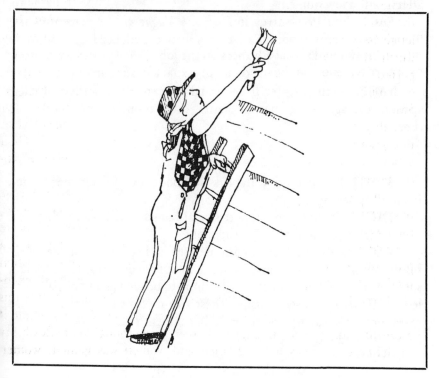

Chapter Three
Myths and Facts

An elaborate series of myths supports all forms of violence against women. These myths, often based on false assumptions about men's and women's "natural" biological make-up, ensure that women who encounter violence against themselves feel guilty rather than violated. Women are therefore less likely to speak up or to take action to eliminate harassment. The following myths, reflecting current attitudes, serve in particular to perpetuate sexual harassment at the workplace.

MYTH: Sexual harassment is not a serious social problem and it affects only a few women.

FACT: In a 1976 survey in *Redbook Magazine,* 88 percent of the 9,000 respondents reported that they had experienced one or more forms of unwanted sexual advances on the job. (See Appendix C for statistical information on the incidence of sexual harassment.)

FACT: Women suffer from sexual harassment regardless of their appearance, age, race, marital status, occupation, or socio-economic class.

MYTH: If women don't speak up about sexual harassment, then it's not happening.

FACT: Women don't report sexual harassment because they feel isolated, guilty, scared of losing their jobs.

FACT: We can begin to eliminate sexual harassment at the workplace only when we share and understand our experiences. If we remain silent, workplace harassment will continue to be seen as a personal problem rather than as a social issue. These two myths will operate until so many women speak up about sexual harassment that our society can no longer pretend it doesn't happen.

MYTH: Women invite sexual harassment by their behavior and/or dress.

FACT: As with rape, sexual harassment is not a sexually motivated act. It is an assertion of hostility and/or power expressed in a sexual manner. Sexual harassment is not women's fault in any way.

FACT: Often women are expected to act or dress seductively both to get and keep their jobs.

MYTH: Only women in certain occupations are likely to be sexually harassed.

FACT: Waitresses, flight attendants, and secretaries are not the only victims of sexual harassment. Women who work in factories, at professional jobs — and all kinds of jobs — consistently report this problem. Students, clients of professionals (doctors, dentists, therapists, etc.), domestic workers, and babysitters also suffer sexual harassment and abuse.

MYTH: Black women are exposed to sexual activity at an early age, are more sensuous and are not as upset by harassment.

MYTH: Asian women are more submissive than other women and would be less likely to be offended by sexual harassment.

FACT: These are patently racist assumptions, and constitute another example of blaming the victim rather than the harasser.

MYTH: It is harmless to harass women verbally on the job or to pinch or pat them. Women who object have no sense of humor.

FACT: Harassment on the job is humiliating and degrading. It undermines a woman's job performance — and often threatens her economic livelihood. Women victimized by sexual harassment suffer emotionally and physically. We should not be prepared to endure degradation with a smile.

MYTH: A firm "no" is enough to discourage any man's sexual advances.

FACT: Because people believe women say no when they really mean yes, men often dismiss women's resistance. Men's greater physical, economic, and social power enables them to override the firmest "no." It should not be women's responsibility to ensure that sexual harassment doesn't happen.

MYTH: Women who remain in a job where they are sexually harassed are masochistic — or are really enjoying it.

FACT: Women's lower socio-economic position in the U.S. means that many are unable to quit their jobs or find new employment.

MYTH: Only bosses are in a position to harass women at the workplace.

FACT: Co-workers and clients can also harass women at the workplace. Clients threaten to withdraw their business. Co-workers make work intolerable. Both complain to the boss —or already have the boss's support.

MYTH: If women can't handle the pressure of the working world, they should stay home.

FACT: Women work out of economic necessity. Staying home is not an option for most working women. Nor — as we know from current publicity on wife abuse — is staying home a protection against sexual harassment.

MYTH: Women make false charges of sexual harassment.

FACT: Women who speak out against harassment meet with negative reactions, ranging from disbelief and ridicule to loss of job. Women have little to gain from false charges.

MYTH: Women sleep their way to "the top" and o▓
of power in the workforce.

FACT: Very few women hold positions of power. For those▓
cases where women have tried to engage in sexual activity to gai▓
motions, evidence shows that it ultimately works against their advai▓
ment. This myth works against a woman who gives in to sexual pressure▓
because she is then mistrusted by fellow workers.

MYTH: Only certain men harass women at work.

FACT: All types of men, in all occupations — whether or not they
hold positions of power — have been reported as harassers.

**MYTH: There are adequate procedures to take care of men who
seriously assault or threaten women at work.**

FACT: Society continues to view sexual harassment from a double
standard. While the sexual harassers are tolerated — boys will be boys
— the women victims bear the brunt of the blame. Personnel managers,
union representatives, human rights agencies, courts, and legislators
reflect these discriminatory attitudes. Women who seek assistance from
these sources to stop sexual harassment are frequently placing themselves at risk of humiliating indifference, ridicule, or even further sexual
insinuation and harassment. Nevertheless, it is important to use these
channels where possible. (See Chapter 9, on legal recourse.)

of women in the work force has changed
____, women aged sixteen and over represented only 29
_____ of the total labor force. By 1978, this number had increased to
41 percent and all projections indicate that the percentage is rising. We
are moving toward an almost equal male/female participation in the
work force. The popular myth that most workers are male is simply no
longer true.

Another myth, the notion that women work for "pin money," or
extra cash, and are not dependent on their earnings for survival, also
must be dismissed in the light of current information provided by the
U.S. Department of Labor. Women work for the same reasons men do
— to provide for their own welfare and the welfare of their families. Of
over 42 million women in the labor force, almost 16 million women support themselves alone or are the sole source of support for a family. If
these women were to lose or quit their jobs, they could not depend on a
husband or a father to insure their, or their family's, survival. Of the
married women who work and whose husbands also work, 5.3 million
contribute to the support of families in which the husbands earn less
than $7,000 annually.

Women whose economic livelihood depends on their jobs do not
have the luxury of quitting when faced with sexual harassment; but it is
surprising how many people ignore this fact when they think about
remedies for sexual harassment. Suggestive comments, passes, touching,
etc. became coercive when refusing sexual attention may mean the loss
of one's job.

The kinds of jobs most women have also affects the nature of sexual
coercion. Clerical work, the largest job category for women workers, includes six out of every ten women in the work force. Clerical workers can
be secretaries, typists, bank tellers, telephone operators, stenographers,
keypunch operators, just to name a few jobs in the clerical category. One
out of five women workers is a service worker. This second largest job
category for women includes waiters, cooks, food counter workers, nurs-
ing aides and private household workers.

Many clerical and service jobs involve providing services such as doing errands, serving food, and arranging "personal business" for a boss or client — activities that have traditionally been associated with a subservient "wifely" role. Also, workers whose jobs include this kind of personal service must often work in isolation — alone with their bosses or clients. An employer has greater opportunity to express desires for sexual activity to his secretary or service worker who is alone with him and performing "wifely" duties.

Although almost half of all men have "blue collar" jobs, only one in seven women are employed this way. Of the 14.7 million women employed in blue collar occupations, the vast majority of them operate machines in factories, leaving a very small percentage as craft workers. As craft workers they tend to be isolated, and in the growing number of situations in which only one or two women are present (on a construction crew, for example), women are especially vulnerable to sexual harassment from supervisors or co-workers. This isolation also exists in the professions, where women find themselves in overwhelmingly male work environments.

Overall Earnings and "Minority" Women

Despite the fact that women are working in record numbers, their average wage in comparison to male workers is declining. In 1955 women's average wage was 64 percent of men's wages. In 1977 it was only 60 percent: the median yearly earnings were $8,600.00 for working women and $14,000.00 for men.

In calculating information about employment of women workers, the U.S. Labor Department includes all races other than white in the category of "minority." Spanish-speaking persons are included in the statistics applying to white populations. The term minority covers black women, Native American women, Asian women, and many other groups, and does not take into account the fact that women of different racial and ethnic groups experience different kinds of problems, especially in relation to work. Certain ethnic groups have a strong cultural prejudice against women taking work outside the home. Some groups experience language problems which put them at a severe disadvantage in their workplaces. Other groups have a long history of racist and sexist exploitation by white masters. These factors shape the frequency and form of expression that sexual harassment will take, as well as women's responses to it.

In 1978, 5.8 million minority women were in the paid labor force, representing almost 55 percent of all minority women in the U.S. Although earnings for minority women have increased in the past twenty-five years, their earnings are still less than that of their white counterparts or of minority men. In addition to this, the unemployment rate of minority women is the highest of any other category (almost 12 percent for women over twenty).*

Low wages, low status occupations and high unemployment among minority women workers directly reflect their perilous economic position. These factors combined with the pervasive racist attitudes of many white employers and co-workers, demonstrate the particular vulnerability of minority women to sexual harassment.

Access to Solutions

When workers have a complaint about their treatment in the workplace or about working conditions, there are very few ways that they can put pressure on their employers. If a federal law is being violated and is enforced through an agency, the employee can begin the long tortured process of agency investigation and prosecution (see legal Appendix B).

Traditionally, the only other "legal" option that can provide pressure or leverage to change working conditions is union action: if a woman worker can get her union to support her complaint about sexual harassment, the union can file a grievance against the employer. As freedom from sexual harassment becomes a basic demand of decent working conditions, unions will be more responsive to complaints filed by women workers in this area. However, although some unions on the national

---

*As with all unemployment figures, this does not represent people who have part-time jobs and are looking for full-time work, or others who are considered underemployed. Many minority women fall into this group. Unemployment figures only show those people whom the government defines as "actively looking for work"; it does not show those who have run out of compensation and are not registered in any official work-seeking bureau.

and local level have shown increasing intere
of most unions has been to ignore it. Even if
union to support a complaint of sexual haras
in 1974 only 21 percent of all workers were ir
percent were in employee associations of an
decreased since 1950. Currently only 11 perc
unions and only another 5 percent are in em
for a majority of women workers, filing a grievance related to sexual harassment is not even a possibility. Most women workers are in small unor-
ganized workplaces and are not able to use their collective power as
workers to fight harassment.

These statistics on women in the workforce reveal women to be in
primarily low status, low paying jobs, with very little autonomy, protection, or control over working conditions. They are considered the most
"replaceable" of all workers, but in reality can little afford to leave their
jobs. These factors combine to make combatting sexual harassment at
the workplace particularly difficult, and have put women workers at the
forefront of an arduous struggle.

Chapter Five

How to Do Outreach Around Sexual Harassment Within Your Existing Target Population

Special outreach and education aimed at the women you define as your target population are a necessary prerequisite to providing services. For the most part, sexual harassment remains hidden, and women often see it as an individual problem. This section suggests ways to announce to your community that sexual harassment is a widespread *social* issue, and that local resources are available to help a woman trapped in a situation of harassment. Each of these suggestions is adaptable to different types of organizations, although not all are suitable for every population.

One of the easiest ways to conduct outreach is to incorporate sexual harassment issues into a program on violence against women or on women and work. If your organization is already involved in either set of concerns, this provides a context to begin exploring women's attitudes about sexual harassment and the extent of the problem locally.

All existing descriptions of your organization — leaflets, stickers, brochures, newspaper listings — should mention sexual harassment information as part of your services. This not only informs women that resources are available, but also raises consciousness that sexual harassment affects many women and is to be taken seriously.

Conduct a survey on the incidence of and attitudes toward sexual harassment at a large workplace in your community. If possible, co-sponsor it with a union or working women's organization. (See Appendix E for sample surveys.) Hold a press conference to announce the findings; at the same time, announce services, programs or workshops available to women in the community who are being harassed or want to work on the issue.

Hold a speak-out where women discuss their experiences with sexual harassment, its effects on women workers, and strategies for eliminating it. Speak-outs raise consciousness, recruit women for rap groups, and organize those who are willing to work with you in developing services.

Use the local media — periodicals, newsletters, radio — to discuss the problem and invite responses.

Organize a coalition of representatives from unions, women's groups, non-traditional employment projects, and workplace associations as a task force to plan large-scale educational campaigns, community-wide surveys, public announcement of harassers, and to develop options for women experiencing harassment. A task force could also sponsor forums or panel discussions as part of its education/outreach.

Link the problem of sexual harassment to other occupational hazards for women. For example, it can be presented as one aspect of a general effort to improve safety on the job for women, or can be linked to harassment experienced by women traveling to and from work, or presented within the context of rights of women workers.

Sponsor discussion/support groups for women on work issues, for women in special types of employment, or for women re-entering or entering the labor force for the first time. Women often discuss sexual harassment as an example of workplace disrespect. Lunch hour programs at or near large workplaces are particularly effective. Street theatre and other visible public events also provoke thought and further action concerning sexual harassment.

Announcement of new services or programs should be targeted to the range of places where working women go — child-care centers, caucuses of workplaces, non-traditional employment training centers, vocational counselors' offices, and neighborhood spots such as laundromats, YWCAs and churches.

Chapter Six

Staff Training Suggestions

Before designing staff training to handle cases of sexual harassment at the workplace, consider such questions as:

• What part is a sexual harassment component to be in terms of your overall program — will it be added to a wide range of present services or is it to become one of a few major emphases?

• How large is the potential population you seek to serve? Does this include all women workers or women in certain occupations or geographical locations?

• Are there class, race, age and/or language differences between your present staff and the women you seek to serve?

• Do you plan to handle the range of sexual harassment cases — from subtle, non-verbal to rape?

• Will your services include information and referral, advocacy with institutions, crisis intervention, long-term follow-up, individual and group support work?

• What kind of balance do you want between direct service, community education, and organizing?

Answering these questions will make it easier to develop a training program that is consistent with your goals. For example, if your main focus is community education, a large part of your preparation will probably involve understanding women's current status in the labor force, legal issues, and myths/attitudes about sexual harassment; compiling referrals may replace in-depth preparation on women's emotional responses to sexual harassment.

The following outline includes basic information to be included in all training sessions, but the distribution of time per topic will vary by previous training and goals of your project. We suggest your training team minimally consist of, or be prepared with, a lawyer or legal worker familiar with workplace remedies, women's rights and rape statutes; and a woman experienced in peer crisis intervention with women who have been victims of violence, Trainers should also have, or be familiar with, a range of work experiences that reflect women's occupations in their area.

I. Definitions of sexual harassment — from the perspectives of women; the courts; the harassers; employers/managers; personnel departments.

II. Sexual harassment within the contexts of violence against women, women and work, and women's position within contemporary society.

III. Myths and attitudes about sexual harassment.

IV. Scope of the problem — survey results nationally and locally (if available).

V. How sexual harassment at the workplace affects all women's lives — commonalities of all women's vulnerability; impact on job security; differences based on factors which affect mobility in the labor force — class, race, sexual preference, age.

VI. Emotional responses of women to sexual harassment; include role plays, case examples.

VII. Peer crisis intervention techniques; and how to run effective rap groups (factors of size, diversity/sameness, group dynamics).

VIII. How to be an effective advocate for a client with institutions.

Chapter Seven

How to Recognize Whether
Your Clients Are Being Sexually Harassed

Case #1

A hispanic teenager nervously stops by a teenage drop-in center. She's having trouble at school. While she had always done fairly well in math before, since she has started taking math from a certain black male teacher, her marks have dropped off seriously. She has started cutting math classes. She has been feeling depressed lately, and her relationships with her family and boyfriend have been rather rocky. Although she seems reluctant to open up, it seems that this male teacher has been asking her what she considers "intimate" questions and has recently cornered her in the hallway and attempted to fondle her. She is very upset, and says she does not understand what she could have done to cause this. She has no idea what to do next.

Case #2

A skilled white female factory worker comes to a local mental health center to discuss her "adjustment" problems at work. This is her first job after several years absence from paid work. She has been through a training program (paid) and is now placed at a factory where she is the only woman in her division. For her four months at work, she has been the target of "practical jokes" and "pranks," as she defines them. She asks: "What's wrong with me? I'm anxious at work and jumpy at home. Maybe I shouldn't be working if I can't learn to be one of the guys, but we really need the money." After further conversation she reveals that these "practical jokers" have been sabotaging her machinery, and presenting her with porno books and sexual accessories.

Case #3

One afternoon a black waitress drops in to the office of a civil liberties organization. She is furious. Her white boss has told her to put out sexually if she wants to keep her job. She's worked there long enough to have flexible hours and some busy shifts which she needs to support herself and her children. The boss also warned her that if she doesn't cooperate, he'll make sure she's not hired elsewhere. She's angry because of the racism; she wants to find another job immediately and needs to get a good job recommendation from her boss.

Case #4

A white woman seeks counseling and assistance from a women's drug and alcoholism rehabilitation center. She has recently developed a fairly serious alcohol problem and is looking for ways to cope with it. Her alcoholism began shortly after she took a new job as a secretary after a long period of unemployment. She admits that her white male boss is an abrasive individual and may in fact be the source of much of her tension. She feels continually insulted and degraded by him. After weeks of counseling, she finally admits that she is worried that his criticism may be stemming from her refusal to see him on a social basis after hours.

Clients of social service agencies, like all women, often experience sexual harassment on the job. Frequently the harassment is not recognized as such. Failure to identify the source of the problem can cause misdirected counseling and can detract from the ability to provide real assistance to clients.

Sexual harassment can go undetected for a variety of reasons. The women themselves may fail to identify their problem as sexual harassment. They may regard sexual advances as an inevitable part of women's lives and therefore seek no solution. They may categorize their problem as one of family, racial, or interpersonal relations, failing to recognize sexual harassment as a form of systematic sexual coercion. Some women who have experienced other forms of violence against women — from rape or battering — may feel they are overreacting. They may feel that having been victimized before, they are now overly-sensitive to sexual advances. Women who do recognize the sexual harassment element of their problem may be reluctant to articulate it, feeling guilty about having "caused" the advance and being unable to stop it. Or they may fear ridicule and reprisals if they speak out.

However, the issue of sexual harassment is beginning to come out of the closet, and as the problem is more openly discussed, women will speak more freely about their experiences. As a result, social services agencies may witness a great increase in the number of such cases.

In any event, it is very important that social service agency personnel who provide services for working women should be conscious of sexual harassment problems and fully capable of providing counseling to sexual harassment victims. They should be on the look-out for changes in women's work histories — past and present. In cases where sexual harassment is the root cause of the woman's problem, or even where it is only one of a number of factors, it would be most helpful if counselors were prepared to open up discussion in a sensitive manner, and assist the woman in finding solutions to her situation.

There are a number of clues or signals that a woman may be encountering sexual harassment. While no one woman is likely to experience all of these problems, the following check list may be useful to agencies seeking to identify sexual harassment elements in particular cases.

Work Situation Affected

- Co-workers, bosses, supervisors, etc. changing behavior toward woman; significant increase or decrease in attention;
- Feels being judged by unclear/unwritten job requirements;
- Feels disrespected at work;
- Undefined job dissatisfaction;
- Changes in job duties or workload or work schedule; demotion, transfer, or firing;
- Can't concentrate or perform usual work tasks effectively;
- Feels out of place at work — "doesn't fit in" because of race, class, religion, sexual preference differences;
- Feels isolated from co-workers' social networks;
- Calling in sick often, coming late to work, taking long breaks and lunch hours;
- Wanting to change jobs;
- Has been fired/laid off.

Other Aspects of Life Affected

- General depression (physical symptoms — changes in sleep or eating patterns, aches and illnesses that incapacitate someone from working, signs of stress);
- Changes in self-concept/self-esteem — particularly feelings of incompetence at handling sexual advances and social situations;
- Changes in social network patterns — i.e., not seeing friends or changing friendship groups, particularly workplace-based;
- Changing attitudes and/or behavior regarding sexual relationships;
- "Short-tempered" with family and/or friends;
- Developing drug/alcohol dependence;
- Seeking lifestyle changes — career choice, living situation.

Chapter Eight
Counseling of Clients

Your Feelings as a Counselor

One thing that has helped us in working with women who have been sexually harassed is to begin by reorganizing the feelings this subject raises in ourselves. We can then try to see how these feelings will affect our interactions with the women who come to us.

One critical issue to deal with before one begins to work with women who have been sexually harassed is to evaluate how sexual harassment itself relates to your life. Are you afraid it might happen to you? Is it already happening to you and this counseling interaction forces you to deal with it? Has it happened to you in the past and you have not resolved it? Do you have some deep-seated notion that a woman must provoke sexual harassment in some way? Does sexual harassment remind you of some other difficult sexual event in your life? Have you experienced a severe assault and might tend to minimize a complaint of chronic subtle harassment? All these questions and many others that

you will be able to discover will affect your interactions with any woman who has been harassed. These are all long term and deep questions but they must be recognized and worked on if we are to deal honestly with clients.

Sexual harassment is a difficult social problem that has no easy solutions and is not going to go away for a long time. The inadequacy of the solutions currently available to us often creates feelings of helplessness and frustration in those of us in AASC. Often we feel inadequate in dealing with clients because we have so few successful options to offer and yet we must deal with the clients' strong feelings of rage, depression or fear. We also find that we must be careful about dealing with too many sexually harassed women at the same time, especially if we want to give clients our time as advocates — going with them to the workplace or to court. One of the hardest things for all of us to do is to set reasonable limits on the number of clients and the amount of time we are prepared to give each one and still feel effective as counselors. For all of these things — feelings of frustration and inadequacy, guilt around setting limits of time and energy with clients, and in dealing with the strong feelings this issue raises in women — we ourselves need support and some place to discuss and share our feelings. If you are preparing to counsel sexually harassed women you should start thinking about where *your* support is going to come from.

Many of us share a common difficulty in talking freely about sex and sexuality. Once we recognize this we can remind ourselves to make an extra effort to raise and discuss the specific sexual nature of any harassment incident if the client wishes to do so. Many of us find it even harder to talk about sex with women who are much older or younger, of a different race, sexual preference or socioeconomic status. Again an extra effort must be made to recognize these difficulties and their effect on our relationships with clients. Another related difficulty we have is a fear that we will put off or intimidate our clients by being too forthright about discussing the sexual aspects of harassing behavior. Our only guide here is experience, but we have found that most people eventually appreciate having an incident or behavior called by its simplest and most direct name, rather than increasing the confusion by use of euphemism or indirect description. A typical example of this is when a client says, "he was fresh with his hands" — you can clarify the situation by asking, "did he touch your breasts?" Often the client is relieved that you are the first one to use an unmistakable sexual word or label. A direct description also seems to make most clients feel more justified in their objections to sexual harassment. One of the biggest difficulties we face in dealing with this issue is the lack of clarity around the exact nature of the offensive behavior, and a euphemism can make a client feel that her complaint is too vague or unjustified.

First Contact *

The basic model of emotional support AASC offers is peer counseling. We are able to offer assistance because we are women who have either experienced sexual harassment personally or are deeply concerned about the causes and manifestations of sexual harassment.

Our first contacts with clients vary enormously. The reactions of women who encounter sexual harassment can fall within a wide range. There are calls from women who feel that they have handled their situation satisfactorily and simply want to share their experiences with us. Other clients are extremely upset, cannot describe their harassment situation clearly, and are unable to work or to function. In working with these women, crisis intervention skills are necessary.

Our experience has been mainly with women who have contacted us because they recognize that they have been sexually harassed, or because they have been referred to us by an agency which has identified the problem as sexual harassment. Clearly, working with this type of client will be very different from working with those who present many issues, one of which may be sexual harassment, but who have not identified sexual harassment as one of their problems. It is important to keep this difference in mind when considering the following summary of our experience.

---

*See Appendix C for sample client intake forms.

Information and Service Referrals

The simplest type of counseling we offer is to the client who requests only specific referrals. She might request the name of a lawyer, a therapeutic referral, information about unemployment compensation or worker compensation, or access to a direct action group which can help in her particular situation.

It is a major responsibility to maintain accurate and up-to-date information and referrals. These must be constantly evaluated on the basis of accessibility and effectiveness. In the case of lawyers and therapists, the first step is to get the names of people who have experience with Title VII or Title IX cases, worker compensation, labor law, or experience working in a non-judgmental way with women in a therapeutic situation.

It is far more difficult to meet the responsibility of getting accurate evaluations of the performance of these individuals and agencies. The best way to do this is to follow up the referral by asking the client her honest opinion of it. Of course, permission to do this must be established with her beforehand, and it may not be suitable in all cases.

Another possibility is to develop a short interview form for each category of referrals, and then meet with the individual therapists, social workers, lawyers, etc., who are being considered. Information about their experience and some subjective sense of their attitudes and practices can be obtained in this manner. (See Appendix D for sample forms for vocational counselors, lawyers, and therapists.) Social service agencies may already have people that work within or in conjunction with their organizations, who can handle these types of referrals. This simplifies matters considerably, but even in these situations, evaluation is extremely important.

Any AASC staffer who is contacted for referral information offers access to other AASC services and information. We try to discuss the harassment situation carefully with the client to make sure that she has no other needs than the ones she has identified.

Difficulties in Talking about Sexual Harassment

It has been our experience that most women find it very difficult to talk about sexual harassment. Part of this is probably due to a certain reserve we all have about discussing anything of a sexual nature with strangers. However, there are other factors operating. Unlike rape, sexual attention is not always unwanted. Clients therefore often find it impossible to make clear to a third party the violation and anger they feel. This same kind of conflict often makes it difficult for a woman to identify the source of stress and unease at her workplace as sexual harassment, especially if this harassment is of the more subtle kind. These difficulties with identification and expression will make the job of the counselor in a social service agency a challenge, particularly if it is the counselor, and not the client, who has identified sexual harassment as a source of stress.

Another reason why women find it difficult to talk about sexual harassment is the enormous amount of self-blame and guilt that harassment provokes. Again the conflict arises in that we all want to be attractive to other people. However, when someone ignores all the negative signals and takes advantage of his power in a workplace by sexually harassing us, we fall into the trap of blaming our normal desire to be noticed and appreciated.

We find that reticence to talk about sexual harassment breaks down quickly once we help the client sort out the difference between wanted and unwanted sexual attention and understand the power dynamic that a sexual harasser uses. It is important that the client examine the power of her sexual harasser. Sexual advances from someone in authority in a work setting or educational institution are very different from sexual advances between equals in a social setting. Sexual harassers in the workforce and in educational institutions understand clearly that women in a subordinate position cannot refuse their attentions without severe repercussions. Once women recognize this, their feelings of guilt and self-blame begin to disappear. It is our experience that one of the most important things we can do at AASC is to get women talking about their harassment situations in ways which are free from self-blame.

Feelings Set Off by Sexual Harassment

The women who call AASC are often extremely upset and disturbed by their harassment. We must first determine whether or not the client is in serious emotional danger and needs to be referred to some kind of psychotherapy. In talking with the client, an AASC staffer may find that the client feels totally isolated from her usual support system — friends, family, etc. She may be unable to discuss her feelings with any of the people she usually talks to. In these cases, we usually try to see how receptive the client will be to a therapeutic referral. Such referrals are most often combined with continuing support and contact from our staff.

The next stage is to try to assemble a coherent picture of the client's situation and to figure out what her most immediate problems are. Is she afraid to return to work? Is she in fear of physical injury from the harasser, or from a family member if they find out about the harassment? Has she been raped? Assaulted? Has she lost her job? Is she extremely depressed and upset about economic survival?

There are some intense and complex feelings that she may be experiencing. Does she blame herself for the harassment situation? Is she upset and guilty? Does the harassment remind her or evoke an earlier sexual abuse situation such as rape, incest, or child abuse? Does the harassment tap into feelings of vulnerability, powerlessness, and alienation from others? Does the client feel betrayed by the harasser whom she might have trusted and looked up to? Does the harassment raise questions about her relationships to other men in her life? All of these are feelings we have discovered in clients who have been deeply affected by the experience of sexual harassment.

A woman who, because of economic or social pressure, has given in to the demands of the harasser, but now feels she wants to end the harassment, will be particularly vulnerable around questions of "blame." For this client, and for the client who has voluntarily been involved with someone in her workplace and is now being harassed and pressured into continuing the relationship against her will, it is extremely important to make it clear that past activities do not control future choices. Another consideration with clients such as these is their alienation from other women in their workplace. Co-workers often do not consider that a woman who is involved with someone at work may have been coerced into this position, or that she may need their support, especially when she wants to end the situation. Too often we accept the mythology that women are "sleeping around to get ahead," and do not consider the possibility that they may have been coerced into a sexual relationship. Clients, of course taking into consideration who they can trust in a workplace, can try to communicate with other women and break down this myth.

We could not begin to list all the issues that sexual harassment raises for a client, but what a counselor can do is to try to help her sort out those problems which are most upsetting to her, and begin to work on some of them.

Basic Procedure: Strategizing a Course of Action

We usually take the client through a few basic steps that we use as standard procedure. The first thing is to make sure that the client realizes that she is not the only one who has experienced sexual harassment. We stress that it is a common problem in our experience, and refer to the situation as an occupational hazard for all women in the workforce. We also stress that no matter how complicated the situation, the client did not bring the harassment on herself. In other words, she is not to blame if she feels she is being harassed. We underscore the idea that unwanted sexual attention is *coercive* and only possible because men as a group have more economic and social power than women.

We then ask the client to evaluate her situation and try to figure out if there are other women who are experiencing this hazard at her workplace. Does the client feel it would be possible to speak with these women without jeopardizing her job? Is there a possibility of getting together to take some kind of action? Could this be a way to start a group, which could deal in an on-going way with these workplace issues?

The next step is to ask the client to write down or mentally outline all of the events leading up to or involving the sexual harassment situation. This helps her to clarify her ideas and feelings. It also helps the counselor to understand the situation. It can help with group activity and discussion or can be used for any organizing or legal action.

Once the situation has been clarified so that the counselor understands what has happened to the client, we outline some of the possible options. It is very important to try to determine what it is that the client really wants to do about the situation.

Most often, what the client wants to do depends on whether she is still on the job, and whether she wants to stay there. (We frequently see harassment victims who are fired for "performance" issues by the employer — employers of course do not list the reason for firing as non-compliance with harassment.) If the client has been fired or has quit because of the harassment, she very often wants information about reinstatement, unemployment, legal redress, and methods of obtaining a decent job recommendation. This client also frequently needs to be assured that she is within her rights in leaving an untenable situation and expecting some sort of redress.

If the client is still in the job and feels she cannot leave it, she usually (but not always) wants to handle the situation with a minimum of public knowledge and legal activity. One of the most frustrating experiences as a counselor is being asked by this kind of client for a simple way of "getting the harasser to stop." We know of no simple way. If the client feels she wants to confront the harasser, we recommend that she does not do it alone. Often, however, the client does not want to involve others and feels that this is the only way for her to go.

In situations such as these our experience has been that the woman's only effective tactic is firm, assertive negative comments about the harassment situation. In a workplace, especially with bosses, one's tendency is to be polite and deferring. Politeness in this kind of situation is often misinterpreted by harassers as acquiescence, and that is the worst possible outcome of a confrontation designed to end the harassment.

So much of this depends on the specific harassment situation and the attitude of the client herself. Many women are in a position where they are isolated and must work very closely with a male boss or co-worker. Their job really depends on how effectively they can work and communicate with this person and they often feel that any confrontation will mean their immediate dismissal. Other women have complicated histories at a particular workplace which they fear will interfere with their ability to confront the harassers.

Differences in Client Response

As to be expected, women from different socioeconomic positions respond differently to sexual harassment and have different ways of coping with the situation. Women with resources and who are familiar with law and business practices, often want legal redress. Women who are not familiar or who have had bad experiences with the legal process, tend to seek other solutions.

Women who have experienced racial discrimination often do not feel the need to separate out the source of their difficulty as sexual harassment. They see it as just one part of being a black woman in the workforce. Women who do not speak English, or for whom English is a second language, are primarily in the most low status, low paying jobs, and can interpret sexual harassment as part of a general condition in which the power structure, primarily white, male, and speaking another language, exploits them. Women from cultures in which work outside the home is a relatively new and perhaps discouraged phenomenon, might internalize this and be quicker to blame themselves when harassed.

A woman entering the workforce for the first time might be overwhelmed by so many new issues to contend with that she will find it particularly difficult to isolate harassment as the source of her difficulties. Others who are new to the workforce might find that when sexually harassed, they start to feel negative about themselves in all aspects of work. Women entering non-traditional fields and encountering sexual harassment might confuse it with the overall general hostility which their presence at a worksite generates. Others might choose not to separate sexual harassment from the general process of initiation that all new workers in non-traditional fields must deal with.

Counselors need to be aware that women from different backgrounds may respond to sexual harassment and perceive their options for action very differently. At AASC, we have found that we are most effective when we encourage each client to explore those options that she herself proposes. Women must take actions that they feel truly comfortable with.

Male Clients

In our three-year experience as a service organization, we have never been contacted by a male client who has been sexually harassed by a woman. We have, however, had several male clients who have been harassed by other men. We maintain a referral list of men's groups and individuals who are willing to talk to men who have been harassed if this is what the client wishes. We also have had AASC staffers, who are all women, work with some of these clients.

We have found that when a man is sexually harassed he experiences the same feeling of violation that women feel. From our limited sample we have noticed that men's immediate response was often anger instead of guilt. Another difference is the added element of homosexuality in these harassment cases. Of course, it is not the homosexuality that is the issue here, but rather the coercive nature of unwanted sexual activity. Given the oppressive societal attitudes toward homosexuality, these clients are even more reticent to discuss their harassment situation with others. It makes it difficult for the client to get together with others in his workplace or to seek some kind of legal redress. The fact that the harasser is male and the client is male may make the usual question of "did I provoke this?" a more complex issue.

The same basic procedures apply to all sexual harassment clients. The most important thing is to get them to talk about the situation, not to blame themselves, and to understand how the harasser is using his power to force the client into something he or she does not want to do.

Chapter Nine
Legal Options

When a woman decides to take legal action against a harasser, she may have several options. Depending on her particular situation, some options will be more feasible than others. Naturally, as with all legal recourse, it is helpful to have as much documentation as possible. It is helpful to have witnesses willing to testify on the woman's behalf. Other victims of the same harasser who are willing to take legal action and a good work record (performance and attendance) will also improve chances for legal success. Proving sexual harassment is a battle, often an unsuccessful one, and women should be prepared for the frustration that may ensue.

Few laws prohibit sexual harassment specifically. At present, sexual harassment is being challenged within the framework of existing sex discrimination laws, workers' compensation legislation, occupational health and safety statutes, criminal and tort law. Because there is no specific inclusion of sexual harassment in these laws, a certain amount of redefinition, reinterpretation, and new analysis is required.

Many of the alternatives we outline below do not work particularly well for sexually harassed women seeking legal redress. Many of them have yet to be tried. We have not indicated how often sexual harassment victims have utilized such avenues successfully, because at this point in time, sexual harassment litigation is still in its infancy. It is just too early to draw any conclusions. What we do know is that there are a variety of potential legal options, none of them have been well-tested, all take long periods of time to pursue, and there is no certainty that the legal result will be satisfactory to the sexually harassed woman.

Nevertheless, sexually harassed women have few other options. Legal action may be the only method they have for pursuing their rights. For some women, a desire to commence legal action may constitute a healthy expression of self-directed activity — a means of fighting back which is necessary to their mental health and sense of self-worth. Also, the more cases are taken to court the more the public will know that sexual harassment occurs.

In counseling clients about taking legal action it is important to inform them that they should consider the following points:

- Litigation takes time.
- Some forms of legal action will require her to hire an attorney, which may be expensive.
- It is important to keep a written record of all incidents relating to sexual harassment as this may be useful evidence.
- A record of all correspondence between a woman and her harasser should be kept.
- In addition to an attorney, it may be helpful to the woman to have a personal advocate to go through the legal process with her to provide emotional support. (It is important for you as a social service counselor to decide whether you have the desire and/or the time to be her advocate. What are your limits?)

The following chart outlines the various legal avenues of which sexually harassed women should be aware. For further details on each legal option, see Appendix D at the end of this book.

Legal Remedy	Brief Description	Types of Benefits	Filing to Settlement	Problems
Title VII — 1964 Civil Rights Act	Federal legislation prohibiting sex discrimination in employment; file with state and appeal through EEOC	Monetary compensation for back pay, lost benefits, and damages; possible job reinstatement	6 months to 1 year on state level; 2-3 years federally	Applies to workplaces with at least 15 employees. Must prove harassment as a form of sex discrimination.
Worker Compensation Act	Operates through State Division of Industrial Accidents. Offers benefits for injury sustained on job.	Weekly wage benefits based on percent of income for period of disability; medical benefits.	Depends on locale; nearer urban area the better; 3 to 6 months with appeal taking 6 months to 1 year longer.	Usually awarded for physical injury; woman must get medical/psychiatric evaluation to be eligible for benefits; company's insurance responsible for settlement.
Occupational Safety and Health Act	Federal Act guaranteeing a "safe and healthful workplace"; allows for inspection of workplace conditions.	Employer fined for violations; responsible for correcting them.	Greatly varies.	Applies to workplaces with at least 15 employees; to date OSHA only used for physical/structural hazards (e.g., toxic substances).
Unemployment Insurance	Award for attributable cause for employment termination due to compelling personal reasons or cause attributable to employer.	Percent of weekly salary up to limit which varies state to state.	Approximately 6 months.	Percent of women's income often too low to meet basic expenses; need minimum income and minimum length of employment; must prove attempt to change work situation by complaining to employer or requesting leave of absence.

Criminal Rape Statutes	Varies state by state; some include degrees of sexual assault.	Conviction and/or imprisonment of harasser/rapist.	Approximately 1 year.	No compensation for woman. Woman's previous sexual history may be admissible in evidence. Only rapists with low socioeconomic status receive prison sentences if convicted. Others often receive suspended sentences and/or court order to seek psychotherapy.
Other criminal sanctions	Assault, battery and other criminal charges may be possible; varies state by state.	Conviction of harasser; fines or imprisonment.	Approximately 1 year.	Similar to rape charges; police reluctant to lay charges with corroboration and witnesses.
Civil Lawsuits	Breach of contract, and various tort lawsuits based on common law.	Financial compensation for employment losses and physical or emotional injury.	Approximately 2-3 years.	Requires women hire a private attorney, legal fees expensive.
Union Grievance Procedure	Breach of union contract allows woman to file grievance with union rep. Union processes case through grievance procedure to arbitration.	Financial compensation for employment losses, reinstatement to job if woman has been dismissed.	Varies from union to union, company to company. Can be settled in weeks or may require arbitration which could take a year.	Few women are unionized; union contract may not be interpreted to cover sexual harassment. Male-dominated unions may be unresponsive.
Title IX Civil Rights Act	Federal legislation prohibiting sex discrimination in education; file with HEW; possibly there is also a private right of action.	Cut-off of federal funding to the educational institution.	Varies regionally; if taken to court can be 1-2 years.	Sanctions appear limited; unclear whether women can utilize a private right of action under Title IX.

Extra-Legal Tactics

In view of the drawbacks and shortcomings of legal options, we find we must develop alternative measures to fight back against sexual harassment. AASC therefore suggests and supports "extra-legal" activities which women might get together to pursue in addition to legal remedies.

"Extra-legal" tactics include:

• Sending a warning letter to the harasser in the name of AASC, which would *not* mention the woman worker's name;

• Negotiating with personnel departments, unions or workplace associations to formulate personnel guidelines or worker contracts which prohibit harassment and outline grievance procedures;

• Leafletting women's bathrooms at work as a warning to other women workers;

• Surveying workplaces for prevalence of harassment as a base for pressuring workplace policy changes;* and

• Picketing harassers' places of employment.

As with any course of action, women must be clear about possible consequences and feel that they can afford these risks.

Other strategies that allow women to take action and raise public consciousness about the issue fall into the category of "pressure group" activities. The targets are existing workplace organizations or associations that have virtually ignored sexual harassment and other problems specific to working women. Unions, for example, must become accountable in their leadership and provide programs to address working women's needs. Sexual harassment as an issue should be incorporated into organizing drives and contract negotiations. Finally, it is vital that workplace harassment be viewed as an occupational hazard affecting most women workers. Occupational Health and Safety Administration, Unemployment Compensation, and the Division of Industrial Accidents (which handles worker compensation cases) can, through education and a steady stream of cases, become aware of and responsive to the seriousness of sexual harassment.

---

*See Appendix E for sample survey.

Appendix A

How Widespread Is Sexual Harassment? Survey Results

A few recent surveys begin to give us a picture of the pervasiveness of sexual harassment, and its effects on working women's lives.

In May of 1975, Working Women United Institute (WWUI) conducted a survey in the Binghamton/Ithaca region of upstate New York on the problem of sexual harassment. Sexual harassment is defined in this survey as "any repeated and unwanted sexual comments, looks, suggestion or physical contact that you find objectionable or offensive and causes you discomfort on your job." Of the 155 women surveyed. 70 percent reported that they had experienced sexual harassment at least once. Ninety-two percent of the respondents considered it a serious problem, and even among those women who had never experienced sexual harassment, 63 percent considered it serious.

In a study conducted by *Redbook Magazine* in 1976, 88 percent of 9,000 respondents had experienced some form of sexual harassment. Ninety-two percent of the total responses considered the problem of sexual harassment "serious."

Of the 875 women and men in professional and clerical positions polled in 1976 by the Ad Hoc Group on Equal Rights for Women at the United Nations, one-half of the women as well as 31 percent of the men reported that they had at some time either personally experienced sexual pressures or were aware that such pressure existed within the organization.

A naval officer used the *Redbook* questionnaire to poll women on his base and in the neighboring town of Monterey, California. Eighty-one percent replied that they had experienced some form of sexual harassment.

As the Working Women United Institute and the *Redbook* surveys indicate, sexual harassment is experienced by women of all ages and occupations, regardless of their salary or marital status. However, the harassment is more severe against women on the lower end of the salary and occupational scale. In the WWUI survey, women who earned a median income of $121 per week, and above, mostly experienced verbal harassment. As the median income dropped to $92 per week, however, the incidence of physical harassment rose. Fifty-six percent of Working Women United Institute's respondents had been subjected to physical harassment.

In the WWUI survey, of the 70 percent who had been sexually harassed, 75 percent ignored it. The harassment only continued or worsened. Twenty-five percent of these women were penalized by unwarranted reprimands, sabotage of their work, and/or dismissal. Only 18 percent of those harassed complained through established channels. No action was taken in over half of the reported cases. In one-third of the cases, negative repercussions such as increased workloads, complaints about the quality of their work, unwarranted reprimands and poor personnel reports resulted.

In this survey, the women who did not complain cited the same reasons: 52 percent felt that nothing would be done; 43 percent felt it would be treated lightly or they would be ridiculed; and 30 percent felt they would be blamed or there would be some repercussions. *Redbook* reports that out of their total respondent pool, only 25 percent think that a harasser who is reported would be "asked to stop — or else." At the United Nations, slightly less than one-third of the staff members who were sexually harassed complained. The reason frequently given for not having done so was the perceived absence of proper channels through which to report. In fact, there is some evidence that this data is accurate: when *Harvard Business Review* polled 1,500 male managers (from its subscribers) on management issues related to women, most of them said they "do not feel their organizations have any responsibility to alter their employees' attitudes towards women."

Rather than complain, it appears that women attempt to escape sexual harassment by altering their way of life. In response to *Redbook*'s question, "How do you shield yourself from sexual harassment?," a majority indicated that they adopt a "cool, guarded manner." Fifteen percent reported to "dressing with extreme modesty."

Both the Working Women United Institute's and *Redbook*'s surveys confirmed the pernicious effect sexual harassment has upon its victims. Forty-eight percent of *Redbook*'s respondents either knew somebody who or they themselves had quit or been fired from a job due to harassment. Seventy-five percent reported being "embarrassed," "demeaned," or "intimidated" by the harassment. Eighty-one percent felt "angry" about the harassment; 50 percent were "upset"; 24 percent — "frightened"; and 23 percent — "guilty." There were also frequent complaints of powerlessness, self-consciousness, feelings of defeat and diminished ambition, decreased job satisfaction, impairment of job performance, and physical symptoms.

What do these survey results mean? The table below summarizes the key findings of surveys discussed above:

	Working Women United	Redbook	United Nations
Date	1975	1976	1976
Number in survey	155 women	9,000 women	875 women and men
Percent experienced harassment	70%	88%	50% women; 31% men experienced or aware of it
Percent considered harassment serious	92%	92%	—
Other findings	75% ignored it	48% themselves or knew of job loss due to harassment	Approximately ⅓ who experienced it reported it

Revealed by the surveys are some important facts:

• The majority of working women have experienced or are aware of sexual harassment at the workplace.

• Sexual harassment seems to escalate from subtle to more blatantly abusive forms.

• Sexual harassment affects women of all job categories, racial and ethnic groups, and ages.

• Most sexual harassment cases remain hidden and unreported.

Thus, we can conclude that the threat and reality of sexual harassment undermine women's job security.

The above survey results are limited by the absence of information about race as a factor in sexual harassment. We can assume that a large number of Third World women are supervised by white men and therefore subject to the threat and reality of harassment that is both racist and sexist in nature. None of the surveys specifically asked questions that would reveal information about whether Third World women are more vulnerable to harassment than white women, about the emotional responses and sense of options held by Black, Hispanic and other Third World women, or about the relationship of sexual harassment to racist myths about women from different racial groups. The history of rape and racism in this country indicates that Black women in particular have had no legal recourse for, or societal support against, their systematic sexual abuse by white men. Future surveys should address this question, because creating viable options for all women workers means understanding the dynamics of harassment as they vary by race, occupation and power relation to harasser.

Appendix B
Legal

As listed in the chart on pp. 40-41, there are a number of possible legal avenues sexually harassed women can pursue. The following will provide some basic information about the various options.

Title VII

Title VII is the section of the 1964 Civil Rights Act which prohibits employment discrimination on the basis of sex. While it is potentially the most extensive sex discrimination legislation to date for working women, different courts have given different effect to its provisions. Some have found sexual harassment to be covered; others have not. Furthermore, it applies only to workplaces with 15 or more employees. In recent years, sexual harassment cases have been won and lost under Title VII in nearly equal numbers.

In any Title VII claim, state and local remedies must be pursued first. The woman must file a complaint with the state arm of the Equal Employment Opportunity Commission (EEOC), which in Massachusetts is the Massachusetts Commission Against Discrimination (MCAD). In other states these state arms of the EEOC are known as human rights commissions. Outside of Massachusetts, contact your local EEOC office to find out what agency applies in your state. All complaints must be filed within 180 days of the alleged violation. If she has lost her job because of sexual harassment, it is possible for a woman worker who is successful at this level to be reinstated in her job and to win back wages amounting to the money she would have earned if she had suffered no discrimination. Back pay can be calculated as far back as two years prior to the filing of the charge.

In such cases it is crucial to prove employer responsibility, that is, that there was an employer policy that promoted the discrimination. This may be difficult to demonstrate since sexual harassment is usually seen as an encounter between individuals. Some courts have required the woman to prove that sexual harassment was a company-designed and oriented policy and practice (obviously an impossible standard to meet). Other courts have been more open to finding employer responsibility, holding that any practice or policy of a supervisor is the practice and policy of the employer. Other courts have looked to see whether the employer knew or should have known of the sexual harassment, or whether the employer acquiesced in the sexual harassment by taking no constructive action against it. It seems fairly well settled that an employer can absolve himself from liability by proving that the sexual harasser acted contrary to company policy, and that the company acted to rectify the consequences once the harasser's actions came to light. Whether or not this means that a sexual harassment victim must complain to higher management inside the company before bringing a Title VII claim is not clear. The argument could be made before the courts that the sexual harassment victim is not required to make an inside complaint unless the employer can show that his organization had policies against sexual harassment and that immediate and satisfactory action would have been taken on any sexual harassment complaints.

Title VII cases usually involve women who have lost their jobs, since this is the most blatant form that employment discrimination can take. A great deal of harassment, however, does not result in an actual firing of the woman. She may be subtly manipulated into resigning through exposure to intolerable working conditions. Title VII refers to this as "constructive dismissal." Women who are forced to quit in this manner are also protected under the Act.

The time period between filing and settlement is six months to one year on a state level. The state agency has 60 days to act on the charge (120 days if the agency has been operating less than a year). If a woman does not meet with success through her state agency, she may appeal to the EEOC, whose backlog of cases dates three years. Therefore, a woman may wait two to five years between filing and settlement.

If a successful settlement cannot be reached, the woman may file a Title VII civil court suit on her own. The EEOC also has the right to file suit on the woman's behalf, but does so rarely. However, the woman's right to sue on her own is fairly broad. Even where the evidence from the EEOC investigation does not indicate a violation of the law, and the EEOC will take no further action, the woman herself has a right to sue. She can also request a right-to-sue letter if the EEOC has not brought suit within 180 days from the original filing of the charge.

Worker Compensation Act

The Worker Compensation Act is designed to offer recompense to a worker either for time (and therefore, earnings) missed on the job due to a work-related injury, or for medical expenses. Companies are insured for such purposes, and it is the insurer of the employer with whom the injured worker negotiates (through the state division of industrial accidents). The injury need not be the sole or initial cause of a complaint; it may merely be an aggravation of an existing condition.

It is conceivable that a woman worker severely distressed by sexual harassment could successfully file a complaint of disability. If she missed work for six consecutive days she may be eligible to collect weekly wage benefits. If she was out of work at least one or two days she may be able to collect medical benefits. Wage benefits are calculated on a percentage of income; the maximum varies from state to state, but it is retroactive to the date the injury occurred. In Massachusetts, the maximum is $150 per week.

Should a woman feel she needs to see a psychotherapist (who must be an M.D.-psychiatrist within the regulations of the Worker Compensation Act) due to the psychological stress of harassment, she may be able to get her employer's insurer to pay for this treatment as well as for any treatment resulting from physical ailments. The more clinical evidence, the stronger the case. Therefore, with the state board administering worker compensation cases, a "well documented" rape or assault stands a better chance than a less obvious form of harassment.

Once a woman files with the Worker Compensation Board, she may expect a conference, which is similar to a hearing, within three months. The time lag here depends upon the locale; in rural areas, women may have a longer waiting period. At this first conference, it may be decided another one is necessary — perhaps because it is a complicated case or because more investigation may be necessary. Any appeal over decisions made at the first or second conference could take six months to a year.

This type of legal recourse would work best with a woman who has been clearly disabled either physically or emotionally, such that she was compelled to seek medical or psychological attention. Unless she suffered some form of physical assault, it is unlikely that she would be awarded weekly wage benefits. If she remains at her job but continues to suffer emotionally from some form of harassment to the point where she is under the treatment of a psychiatrist, she may be able to win payment for those expenses.*

The lengthy negotiation procedure is a weighty consideration when contemplating this avenue. If a woman may have a wait of a year or longer for a decision, how does she support herself or pay her medical bills in the meantime?

Occupational Safety and Health Act

Sexual harassment at the workplace can be interpreted as an occupational health hazard. Whether faced with chronic verbal or physical harassment or temporary abuse, women workers suffer emotionally and physically from such attacks.

One legal tactic is to file a complaint with the Occupational Safety

---

*A recent decision of the Massachusetts Supreme Judicial Court (Albanese v. Atlantic Steel Co., Everett, May 4, 1979) gives cause for much greater optimism about this legal option. The court awarded compensation to Joseph Albanese, who was totally disabled as a result of mental illness related to a series of emotionally stressful work-related incidents. Although this one did not involved disablement due to stress created from sexual harassment, its holdings will serve as a useful precedent for sexually harassed women in the future.

and Health Administration (OSHA), charging emotional and/or physical damage as a result of sexual harassment. The Occupational Safety and Health Act of 1970 guarantees a "safe and healthful workplace" to working people (when there are 15 or more employees, that is). The Act itself mandates inspection of workplace conditions and permits any worker to file a complaint and request an inspection, while protecting the worker from reprisal for doing so. But, "as with so many laws, the Act guarantees many rights to the American worker, but the enforcement of the law to obtain these rights is in fact a daily battle against both the government and industry."*

This legislation has previously been utilized largely to protect workers from physical dangers, such as exposure to chemicals and faulty building conditions. Although there may be some difficulties in trying to have this legislation extended to cover sexual harassment, OSHA complaints remain an important option. If a woman worker has suffered chronic or acute stress due to sexual harassment in the form of such physical symptoms as weight change, headaches, skin rashes, nervousness, etc., OSHA *may* find the employer in violation of providing a healthy working environment. To our knowledge, however, occupational safety and health regulations have not as yet been applied in sexual harassment cases. Encouragingly, the *Encyclopedia of Occupational Health and Safety*† defines "stress" broadly, including situations which are "interpreted as a threat to the goals, integrity, or well-being of the individual." Sexual harassment clearly falls within this definition.

Any beneficial consequence of seeking this legal recourse would, unfortunately, take time. The delay between filing and the ultimate decision varies according to the state enforcing bureau and the particular case. Penalties for violations are also discouraging, "generally averaging less than $30 per violation."‡ However, although the penalty is low it is important that sexual harassment be recognized as an occupational hazard for working women.

---

*Stellman, Jeanne Mager, Susan Daum, *Work Is Dangerous to Your Health*. New York: Vintage Books, 1973, p. 7.

†The *Encyclopedia* is a standard, widely-accepted reference text compiled by the International Labor Organization of the United Nations. OSHA has in the past given its definitions due consideration.

‡*Ibid.*, p. 185.

Unemployment Insurance

If a woman feels compelled to quit her job because she has been sexually harassed, unemployment insurance is a possibility. However, it requires a strong case and a willingness to be patient with the procedures. Additionally, to be eligible, one must either have earned money for at least 15 weeks out of the last year, or have earned over $3,240 in two calendar quarters in the previous year.

There are two ways a worker can get benefits under the Massachusetts law. The first is if a person left "for good cause attributable to the employing unit." The second is if one quit for "compelling personal reasons," which are defined as moving and having no available means of transportation, illness or death of a family member, etc. For sexual harassment at the workplace, only the first is applicable since the employer must be proven at fault. To win benefits a woman must prove that she has tried to change her work situation, either by complaining to her employer — preferably in writing or with witnesses — or by requesting a leave of absence which was denied.

It may take six to eight months to win unemployment insurance on the grounds of sexual harassment. However, Wisconsin recently passed positive legislation in this area, making it clear that unemployment compensation can be awarded to an employee who quits a job because of sexual harassment.

Criminal Statutes

The serious limitations of using criminal rape statutes as a means of protecting women from sexual assaults are by now well known. Most rape laws apply only to "forced vaginal penetration," and not to less violent but equally destructive forms of sexual harassment. Court procedures are long, emotionally draining, and rarely result in convictions. Any history of workplace interaction between the rapist and the woman is most likely admissible evidence; and there is no compensation for the woman besides a possible conviction of the rapist. Furthermore, the racism, classism, and sexism of the criminal justice system present serious dilemmas in the use of this option. White, economically advantaged rapists, if convicted, often receive suspended sentences and/or a court order to seek psychotherapy.

In cases where sexual harassment falls short of actual rape, a number of other criminal charges are possible. Assault and battery are punishable crimes under all state criminal statutes. "Assault" and "battery" are not always described the same way in all states, but in general they can be defined as follows:

"Battery" is the unlawful application of force (either through bodily injury or offensive touching) to the person of another, without that person's consent.

"Assault" is an attempted battery, or intentional frightening. It involves threatening conduct which is intended to frighten or injure, and succeeds in causing the victim to have a reasonable apprehension of immediate bodily harm.

Other criminal charges might possibly include: attempted rape, assault with intent to commit rape, aggravated assault, extortion. Since each state has its own criminal legislation, sexual harassment victims and their advocates should examine their own state's statutes to determine exactly what offenses could be charged. Police officers generally refuse to lay criminal charges in sexual harassment cases unless the woman can provide corroboration and witnesses. Women have the option of filing criminal complaints themselves, but the court system tends to treat these without much seriousness. Additionally, in all criminal prosecutions, the accused must be proved guilty "beyond a reasonable doubt." This standard of proof is much higher than the "balance of probabilities" test* used in non-criminal litigation.

Civil Lawsuits

Tort and contract lawsuits can be brought by a woman against an individual harasser, his company, or both, in civil court, under a variety of legal doctrines. To name a few, a woman can sue for breach of an employment contract, for intentional infliction of mental duress suffered from harassment, or for illness or injury due to an assault. This route has the advantage of allowing a woman to control the legal proc-

---

*In criminal law, the prosecution must convince the judge and jury that the accused is guilty beyond a reasonable doubt. In a civil suit, the plaintiff must convince the jury only that his or her version of the facts is true on a balance of probabilities — a test much closer to a 50-50 balancing.

ess. She may decide when to take legal proceedings, and when to discontinue them. She is not subject to the whim of governmental agencies, police officers, or district attorneys.

Since this takes place in civil, not criminal, court, a woman is awarded a monetary settlement for damages if her suit is successful. These damages may be for physical or emotional injury, expenses in looking for a new job, loss of employment benefits, loss of pay if she was unable to work or was fired, transferred or demoted, or the difference in pay between her new and her old job.

It can be an expensive remedy whether or not the woman wins, since a private attorney is necessary and fees generally average one-third of the settlement award. Some attorneys, however, will take payment only where the woman wins (the contingency fee arrangement) and not if she loses. It can take time as well — anywhere from two to three years — unless it is settled out of court.

Unionization and the Grievance Procedure

Unionized employees should have a great deal more power in fighting sexual harassment than their non-unionized counterparts, although there are limitations to this approach as outlined in Chapter 4. Once a union has acquired bargaining rights, employees no longer bargain with management on a one-to-one basis. Management no longer has the prerogative to issue edicts covering wage levels, fringe benefits, discipline, and dismissal. Instead, the union acts as the employees' agent, bargaining for them on a collective basis. Between management and the union, a binding contract is agreed to which sets out pay levels and usually stipulates that the employer can discipline and discharge employees only "for just cause." Some unions have bargained contracts which prohibit sexual harassment specifically.

A grievance procedure is set up to settle the dispute whenever an employee alleges that a contract has been breached. A sexually harassed woman must lodge a grievance complaint with her union representative. The complaint is generally heard at various levels of appeal within the organization. The union always acts as the employee's advocate. If the dispute is not resolved, it is ultimately heard by an impartial, outside arbitrator, who is chosen jointly by management and the union. Again, the union will act as the woman's advocate, hiring legal counsel at its own expense where required. If the arbitrator determines that sexual harassment has involved a breach of the contract, back-pay can be awarded and the woman can be reinstated to her job.

Title IX

If someone in school experiences sexual harassment, she may be protected by Title IX of the Civil Rights Act. This legislation reads:

> No person in the U.S. shall, on the basis of sex, be excluded from participation in, be denied the benefits of, or be subjected to discrimination under any educational program or activity receiving federal financial assistance.

Under this law federally funded school districts must appoint a Title IX coordinator to ensure that the law is implemented. Women can ask any school official about how to contact this person. It is to be hoped that this coordinator will be sensitive to the problem of sexual harassment. The coordinator is appointed as the woman's advocate and can explain her legal rights.

Under Title IX, institutions receiving federal financial assistance must adopt grievance procedures for complaints of sex discrimination, although individuals may opt not to use the procedures and can file directly with the U.S. Department of Health, Education, and Welfare (HEW). Once the HEW receives a charge, it is required to investigate and conduct a hearing to determine whether the school discriminates.

If the result of this hearing is not acceptable to her, a woman can ask a U.S. Court of Appeals to review the HEW action. The only sanction the HEW has available under Title IX is the cut-off of federal funds to the school. The woman is not awarded damages, and the school cannot be ordered to stop discriminating.

The courts have not yet conclusively decided whether a woman has the right to bring a private court action based on a breach of Title IX. Decisions to date go both ways, although cases are now pending which may determine this point. Obviously, a private lawsuit entails costs — attorney's fees, time delay, etc. However, under the Civil Rights Attorneys' Fees Awards Act, the courts may award attorneys' fees to a woman who is successful in a Title IX action.

To date there have been no decisions under Title IX on sexual harassment. However, there is currently at least one case pending (the Yale University lawsuit), in which the plaintiffs are attempting to argue that Title IX is a basis for eliminating sexual harassment. Although the decision in this case is not yet in, this may become a hopeful avenue.

by Loret Ulmschneider

Appendix C
Sample Client Intake Sheet

AASC member(s) involved _____

How contacted: ☐ phone ☐ mail ☐ other _____

Information about victim:

Name _____ Age _____ Race _____ Job _____

Address _____ Phone number_____

Information about harasser:

Name _____ Age _____ Race _____

Job _____Phone number_____

Date of incident _____ Type of workplace _____

Name of workplace _____

Description of the incident (including relationship between two; how long harassment continued; other victims?)

_____

_____

_____

Reported? ☐ yes ☐ no If so, to whom? _____

Any assistance given? ☐ yes ☐ no If so, what kind? _____

_____

Any retaliation? ☐ yes ☐ no If so, what kind? _____

_____

Emotional response of victim _____

Action victim wants from AASC _____

Other options victim identifies _____

_____

AASC response given _____

_____

Plans for follow-up, additional comments _____

Appendix D

Sample Evaluation Forms for Vocational Counselors, Lawyers, and Therapists

VOCATIONAL COUNSELOR EVALUATION FORM

Date contacted: _____

Name of organization/agency _____

Name(s) of counselor(s) _____

Address _____

Phone number _____

What kind of skills do you expect women to have (e.g., educational or job skill requirements)?

What kind of interview procedures or techniques?

Sensitivity to sexism, sex-segregated jobs, sexual harassment. What has been your experience with sexism in placing women in jobs? What kinds of attitudes do you find prevalent with employers (toward women)? If you had a woman who had just been sexually harassed on her previous job, would and how would you be sensitive to it?

How do you aid women in job decisions or career changes?

What kind of resources do you offer (e.g., job files, contacts, relations with other agencies)?

What are the kinds of possible job placements you offer?

Do you charge a fee and to whom (employer or employee)? How much?

Do you offer workshops or training programs?

How sensitive are you to helping a working mother find a job (in terms of hours, etc.)? Do you help in finding jobs that provide day care?

Do you encourage acquiring new job skills (paid while training)?

Any follow-up procedures?

Additional comments:

LEGAL REFERRAL EVALUATION FORM

Date contacted: _____

Name of organization / firm _____

Address _____ Phone _____

Name(s) of lawyer(s) / legal worker(s) _____

Organization's specialization(s) _____

Eligibility requirements (residence, income, type of case, etc.) _____

_____

Fees _____

Has your organization handled cases of violence vs. women (rape, battered wives, etc.)?

_____

How are cases handled — do clients see intake workers, legal researchers, and/or lawyers? _____

What is your group's philosophy about the criminal justice system, particularly in relation to women (i.e., where do legal reforms fit into your general view)? _____

_____

Do you feel that all victims of violent crime should report to the police? _____

_____

Do you see inadequacies in the existing rape laws? _____

If yes, what would model legislation include? _____

_____

What are your views on penalties/treatment for convicted "sex offenders"? _____

_____

Would you be interested in working on test cases around workplace harassment?

class actions _____ labor _____ Title VII _____

civil _____ criminal _____ OSHA regs _____

other _____

Are skills courses and/or workshops available from members of your group? _____

_____

Evaluator(s) comments:

GUIDELINES FOR EVALUATING MENTAL HEALTH RESOURCES

Name of organization/agency _____

Address _____

Phone _____ Contact person _____

Estimate of age _____ Counselors _____

1. Talk about AASC.

2. Are you interested in being a referral person? _____ What procedures would you like us to follow (i.e., shall we call you or have the woman call you directly)? _____

3. Background experience that might make you a good referral person for us (training, therapeutic orientation, experience with women/women's groups). _____ _____ Access to medication? _____

4. Have you or your agency had any experience in dealing with women who have been sexually harassed and/or raped? _____

5. What would you consider to be common reactions of rape victims? _____ _____

   Why would you say that? _____

6. What are your fees ?_____

   Do you accept medicaid patients? _____

   Are you reimbursible by insurance? _____

   Do you have a sliding fee scale and what is the range? _____

7. What are your hours? _____ Do you have a waiting list? _____

8. Are there any restrictions as to the women you service (i.e., they must live in a certain area)? _____

9. What types of counseling do you provide (i.e., individual, group, couples and/or family)? _____

10. What is your policy in dealing with lesbians and minorities? _____ _____

11. How would you respond to a woman who has been raped at the workplace and does not wish to report it to the police? _____

12. Can you suggest any other therapists or centers that would be good referrals? _____ _____

13. Would you like a consultant from our group to come and talk with you and/or your staff? _____

Personal response and reactions of AASC interview. (Note any signs of racism, classism, etc. Was the person warm, open and how easy were they to relate to?)

Appendix E

Sample Survey Forms:
Redbook, High School Students,
Health and Safety

SEXUAL HARASSMENT QUESTIONNAIRE
SAMPLE FOR HIGH SCHOOL STUDENTS

Sexual harassment takes many forms. It includes verbal harassment or abuse, subtle pressure for sexual activity, as well as rape and attempted rape. To refuse sexual demands from a teacher, administrator, counselor or other school personnel means the risk of lowered grades, unfavorable recommendations for jobs or colleges, or other punitive measures. There are possible legal remedies for a student in this situation, including child abuse legislation, Title IX, civil suits and criminal charges for rape, statutory rape, attempted rape or assault.

All information provided by you on this questionnaire is strictly confidential, and will not be used against you. The more accurate information we have about the threat and reality of sexual harassment of students, the better able we will be to provide remedies.

For questions with multiple answers, please check as many as apply.

Please indicate your sex: Male ☐   Female ☐

Age _____ Race _____ Year in school _____

1. Please define what you think sexual harassment means.

2. Have you ever received any sexual attention from any school personnel while attending high school, junior high school, or grammar school?

   yes ☐   no ☐   Which school(s)? _____

If you have experienced sexual attention more than once, please fill out the following questions for the *more recent* experience. If you have never experienced sexual attention or harassment, please answer as many of the following quesns as you can as to what you think you would do in the situation, and how you think you would feel.

3. What position (teacher, administrator, counselor, etc.) does this person hold?

   _____ Does s/he have tenure? yes ☐   no ☐

   Age of harasser _____ Race of harasser _____

4. How did you feel about the attention?
   ☐ angry
   ☐ scared
   ☐ confused
   ☐ ashamed
   ☐ I thought the attention was misunderstood by me
   ☐ I was flattered
   ☐ I didn't think it was a big deal
   ☐ it was just a sexist attitude
   ☐ other (specify) _____

5. What form did the sexual attention take?
   ☐ staring
   ☐ gestures
   ☐ remarks made in front of others
   ☐ remarks made in private
   ☐ touching
   ☐ atmosphere / vibes
   ☐ explicit proposition
   ☐ other (specify) _____

6. Where did the attention take place?
   ☐ classroom
   ☐ car (if he offered you a ride home)
   ☐ auditorium
   ☐ parking lot
   ☐ teachers' lounge
   ☐ cafeteria
   ☐ office
   ☐ hallway
   ☐ gym or locker room
   ☐ other (specify) _____

7. When did the attention take place?
   ☐ after school
   ☐ before school
   ☐ between classes
   ☐ during class
   ☐ during lunch or recess
   ☐ in the evening
   ☐ other (specify) _____

8. Did you ever discuss the events that occurred to you with a third party?
   - ☐ friend (please describe friendship and age) _____
   - ☐ teacher
   - ☐ guidance counselor
   - ☐ parent
   - ☐ boyfriend/girlfriend
   - ☐ family member
   - ☐ school staff or administrator
   - ☐ community group (please describe) _____
   - ☐ church
   - ☐ agency (e.g., hotline, community mental health center) specify _____
   - ☐ other (specify) _____

9. What did you do about it?
   - ☐ I ignored it
   - ☐ went along with him/her (if so, explain) _____
   - ☐ talked to a teacher or counselor I felt close to
   - ☐ reported him to the principal
   - ☐ cut his class
   - ☐ didn't go to school for a couple of days
   - ☐ transferred to another class
   - ☐ transferred to another school
   - ☐ quit school
   - ☐ talked alone to harasser
   - ☐ slapped or hit harasser
   - ☐ talked with group to harasser
   - ☐ talked with parents to harasser
   - ☐ other (specify) _____

10. If you reported him/her to another teacher, counselor, principal, administrator, how did they react?

    What were the suggestions or actions they recommended?

    Which of these helped?

11. How did you feel about the action you took?

12. After some time elapsed, how did you feel about the incident?

13. Did the way you responded to the attention change the relationship between you and the harasser? If so, explain. yes ☐   no ☐

14. Did the harassment change your relationship with you and any of the following?
    ☐ parents
    ☐ girlfriend/boyfriend
    ☐ friends
    ☐ other school personnel (specify) _____
    ☐ other (specify) _____

15. Did the harassment change the relationship between you and the person(s) you reported to? yes ☐   no ☐   If yes, please explain in what ways.

16. If you went along with the sexual attention, what were the main factors that determined your response?
    ☐ grades
    ☐ I like him/her
    ☐ I need a good recommendation for college
    ☐ I need a good job recommendation
    ☐ s/he was popular with the kids
    ☐ made me feel important
    ☐ made me feel loved
    ☐ I thought it would help my popularity
    ☐ other (specify) _____

17. If you didn't go along with it, what were the main factors determining your response?
    ☐ I didn't like him/her
    ☐ s/he was too old
    ☐ I was afraid someone would find out
    ☐ I was offended/disgusted
    ☐ I didn't think anyone would believe me
    ☐ I was not sexually interested in the harasser

18. Did s/he imply you could get a special favor if you went along with his/her attention? If so, what?

19. Did s/he imply you would be penalized if you would not go along with the attention? yes ☐   no ☐

20. Did he threaten you with any school punishment?
    ☐ suspension
    ☐ disciplinary action
    ☐ drop in grade
    ☐ smear your reputation/tell lies about you
    ☐ phone call to your parents — lying or smearing your reputation
    ☐ other (specify) _____

21. Did the harasser ever make suggestive comments about your body or clothing?
    yes ☐   no ☐   If yes, please explain.

22. How often has this person verbally or physically harassed you sexually? Please indicate number and frequency of times.

23. Does the harasser in question have a reputation of sexually harassing students?
yes ☐   no ☐

24. How do you think a situation like sexual harassment in the schools should be dealt with?
☐ legal action
☐ ignore it
☐ anonymous grievance procedures
☐ teacher or administrator suspension or firing
☐ peer support groups
☐ let individuals deal with it in their own way
☐ knowledge and availability of support within the school
☐ knowledge and availability of support within the community
☐ other (specify) _____

25. Are you aware of sexual harassment going on in your school? yes ☐   no ☐
If yes, how widespread, do you think the problem is?

26. If you have been harassed sexually by a school personnel member, please describe it.

Please give us any additional information or comments about this questionnaire or about the problem of sexual harassment.

HEALTH AND SAFETY QUESTIONNAIRE

Introduction

Women in industries that have been traditionally male dominated are facing problems that have not been part of their previous job experiences. Many of these problems result from either the conditions of the job or the attitudes of their co-workers or employers. From changing job categories and shifts, from sexual harassment to physical abuse, from nasty remarks to unreasonable job demands — women are being harassed and discriminated against. Minority women are subjected to the additional harassment of discrimination and racism.

The WREE Clearinghouse on Blue Collar Women is set up to gather, document, and publicize information about these problems. Your participation in this project will enable us to obtain the wide coverage of problems of blue-collar women that is needed to present to government agencies, legislators, unions, and community organizations so that we can achieve the laws nationally that will give us the protection we demand.

Instructions

The questions in our survey are based on the reports, letters, and stories in the press that have been sent to us by our members and friends. Obviously, we cannot anticipate all the forms that harassment and discrimination may take. We therefore urge that you include as much information as possible. We know that some forms of harassment are subtle and difficult to describe, some are "unpin-downable" as leers, or nasty looks... but they are as painful and uncomfortable to take as more overt actions or remarks. Your name will not appear on any documents made public or in any reports issued without your permission.

Please describe the conditions and forms of harassment and racism as fully as possible. Use additional paper to make your response as lengthy as you wish to describe your life on the job. Refer to the question number if the additional information is in response to a question in the survey. Send for additional copies of the questionnaire to give to your friends and co-workers.

1. Are you the only wage earner in your immediate family? yes ☐   no ☐
   If no, how many workers in family? _____

2. Industry _____ Department _____
   Company (name and location) _____

3. Unions at your plant: 1. _____ 2. _____

4. Are you a union member? yes ☐   no ☐

5. Your job title _____ years on job _____

6. Years at this kind of work _____ Years with company _____

7. Previous job (if any) with same company _____

8. Your apprenticeship training was
   ☐ none
   ☐ company-provided   how long _____
   ☐ union program   how long _____
   ☐ government program   how long _____
   ☐ my own initiative   how long _____
   ☐ other (explain) _____

9. Do you feel your training was adequate? yes ☐   no ☐

10. Were you treated fairly during training? yes ☐   no ☐   If no, explain ____
   _____

   _____

11. Is your kind of work done by men too? yes ☐   no ☐
    Is your pay the same as men get with same time on similar job as you?
    yes ☐   no ☐   If no, show differences _____
    _____

    _____

12. Are you required to do work that men in similar jobs are not required to do?
    yes ☐   no ☐   If yes, explain _____
    _____
    _____

13. Are you required to be equal to men in physical strength, speed, or endurance on
    your job? yes ☐   no ☐   If yes, explain _____
    _____

14. How many women in your job category? _____Men? _____
    How many women in your plant? _____Men? _____
    How many women in your department? _____Men? _____

15. Indicate type of harassment or discrimination and describe each, if you wish
    ☐ racial _____
    ☐ sexual _____
    ☐ physical violence _____
    ☐ violent language _____
    ☐ threats of firing or transfer _____
    ☐ insults/innuendos _____
    ☐ dirty tricks _____
    ☐ false reports on your work _____
    ☐ unfair ratings _____
    ☐ unusual assignments or extra work _____
    ☐ mandatory overtime _____ hours per week _____
    ☐ other, please describe _____
    _____

16. Have you experienced harassment or discrimination on the job by
    ☐ foreman or boss?   yes ☐   no ☐
    ☐ male co-workers?   yes ☐   no ☐
    ☐ clerical staff?   yes ☐   no ☐
    ☐ personnel office?   yes ☐   no ☐
    ☐ others on job? (be specific, please) _____

17. Are there poor facilities? yes ☐   no ☐ If yes, please indicate type of facility and
    describe each, if you wish
    ☐ toilets _____
    ☐ restrooms _____
    ☐ locker rooms _____
    ☐ lunchrooms _____
    ☐ other, please describe _____

18. Are there unsafe or unhealthy conditions? yes ☐   no ☐ If yes, indicate type of condition and describe each, if you wish.

☐ inadequate guards on machines _____

☐ no goggles or other protection _____

☐ poor lighting _____

☐ polluted air _____

☐ dangerous chemicals _____

☐ dangerous speedup _____

☐ bad footing _____

☐ weak bracing or structures _____

☐ other, please describe _____

19. Are there difficult work conditions? yes ☐   no ☐ If yes, indicate type and describe each, if you wish.

☐ heavy loads _____

☐ inadequate or no aids such as dollies, tools, lifts, jacks, etc. _____

☐ uncomfortable room temperatures _____

☐ unbearable noise _____

☐ dirt _____

☐ inadequate workclothes _____

☐ other, please describe _____

20. Do you work shifts? yes ☐   no ☐
Do shifts change? yes ☐   no ☐
Is this a hardship for you? yes ☐   no ☐   If yes, why? _____
_____

21. Does company provide pregnancy and/or maternity benefits? yes ☐   no ☐
If yes, do you feel they are adequate? yes ☐   no ☐

22. Has company cancelled benefits or working conditions you should have?
yes ☐   no ☐   If yes, describe specifically _____
_____

23. Do you need child care for children? yes ☐   no ☐
If you have children, how are they cared for while you work?
☐ babysitter or relative
☐ day care center
☐ unattended
☐ other, please describe _____

24. Any other harassment, complaints, suggestions, etc.
_____
_____

Name _____ Age _____

Address _____

City _____ State _____ Zip _____

Nationality/race _____

Single _____ Married _____ Divorced _____

Number of children _____ Ages _____

Other dependents _____

THE REDBOOK QUESTIONNAIRE

1. What is your occupation?
   - ☐ professional with advanced degree (for example, doctor, lawyer)
   - ☐ teacher, counselor, social worker, nurse
   - ☐ managerial, administrative, business
   - ☐ white-collar (sales, clerical, secretarial)
   - ☐ artist, writer
   - ☐ technician, skilled worker
   - ☐ semiskilled or unskilled worker
   - ☐ other

2. Are you working at present for pay outside the home?
   - ☐ Yes, I have a full-time job (30 or more hours a week).
   - ☐ Yes, I have a part-time job (less than 30 hours a week).
   - ☐ No, I do volunteer work.
   - ☐ No, but I have worked in the past.

3. Which of the following have you experienced with male co-workers or supervisors?
   - ☐ leering or ogling
   - ☐ sexual remarks or teasing
   - ☐ subtle sexual hints and pressures
   - ☐ touching, brushing against, grabbing, pinching
   - ☐ invitations to a date with the implication that refusing may count against you
   - ☐ sexual propositions, with the implication that refusing may count against you
   - ☐ sexual relations, with the implication that refusing may count against you
   - ☐ other forms of sexual harassment
   - ☐ no sexual harassment at all

4. Which one of the following statements best reflects the way you feel?
   - ☐ Sexual tensions between men and women who work together are natural.
   - ☐ Innocent flirtations make the workday interesting.
   - ☐ An attractive woman has to expect sexual advances and learn to handle them.
   - ☐ Encouraging the boss' sexual interest is often a way of getting ahead.
   - ☐ Women who are bothered by male co-workers are usually asking for it.
   - ☐ Unwelcome male attentions on the job are offensive.

5. If a male co-worker or supervisor has made sexual advances to you, how did you feel about it?
   - ☐ It was embarrassing.
   - ☐ It was demeaning.
   - ☐ It was intimidating.
   - ☐ It was flattering.
   - ☐ It was a way of keeping me, a woman, "in my place."
   - ☐ It was of no consequence.
   - ☐ not applicable

6. At work have you ever used your sexual attractiveness for any of the following purposes?
   - ☐ to improve relations with a male supervisor
   - ☐ to catch the attention of higher-ups
   - ☐ to get out of the chores I dislike
   - ☐ to obtain special help from men
   - ☐ to maneuver into a better job position
   - ☐ to obtain other advantages
   - ☐ not applicable

7. What do you think of a woman's using her sexual attractiveness to gain job advantages?
   - ☐ It's only natural — sexual attractiveness is a basic asset meant to be used.
   - ☐ It's a woman's answer to the way men gain job advantages (in locker rooms, on the golf course).
   - ☐ It tends to perpetuate a system of sexism.
   - ☐ It's her own business and it just has nothing to do with me.

8. In getting your job how important do you think your physical attractiveness was?
   - ☐ more important than my other qualifications
   - ☐ equally important
   - ☐ less important
   - ☐ unimportant

9. At work how important is a man's physical attractiveness?
   - ☐ as important as a woman's
   - ☐ less important
   - ☐ more important
   - ☐ unimportant

10. If a male co-worker or supervisor has made sexual advances to you, how did you react?
    - ☐ I enjoyed it.
    - ☐ I ignored it, hoping it would stop.
    - ☐ I worried that if I objected, it would somehow go against me.
    - ☐ I played along with it, hoping it would lead to a promotion.
    - ☐ I asked the man to stop it.
    - ☐ I reported it to a supervisor or a union representative.
    - ☐ not applicable

11. If you were to report a man's unwelcome attention to a supervisor or union representative, what do you think would happen?
    ☐ Nothing at all.
    ☐ I would be told not to take it so seriously.
    ☐ The man would be asked to stop — or else.
    ☐ I would be labeled a "troublemaker."
    ☐ I would be offered a job in another department to help me avoid the man.
    ☐ I would be moved to another department in retaliation.
    ☐ I would be fired.

12. How would you feel if you saw sexual advances being made to another woman at work?
    ☐ I would sympathize with her.
    ☐ I would blame her.
    ☐ I would envy her ability to make sexual attractiveness work for her.
    ☐ I would think nothing of it.

13. How do you feel about sexual harassment?
    ☐ It is a serious problem.
    ☐ It is a minor problem.
    ☐ It is of no importance at all.

14. Have you or any woman you know ever:
    ☐ quit a job because of sexual harassment?
    ☐ been fired because of sexual harassment?
    ☐ not applicable.

15. How do you shield yourself from sexual harassment?
    ☐ I pretend not to notice.
    ☐ I act silly and childish.
    ☐ I adopt a cool, guarded manner.
    ☐ I dress with extreme modesty.
    ☐ I flaunt my wedding ring.
    ☐ I've never had to cope with it.

16. What is your approximate annual salary?
    ☐ less than $5,000
    ☐ $5,000 to $10,000
    ☐ $10,001 to $15,000
    ☐ $15,001 to $25,000
    ☐ more than $25,000

17. What is your age?
    ☐ under 20
    ☐ 20 to 24
    ☐ 25 to 29
    ☐ 30 to 35
    ☐ over 35

18. What is your marital status?
    ☐ single
    ☐ living with a man
    ☐ married, first time
    ☐ remarried
    ☐ separated
    ☐ divorced
    ☐ widowed

19. What is the highest level of education you have completed?
    ☐ grade school
    ☐ high school
    ☐ some college
    ☐ college graduate
    ☐ some graduate work
    ☐ advanced degree

20. Where do you live?
    ☐ New England
    ☐ Middle Atlantic states
    ☐ South Atlantic states
    ☐ North Central states
    ☐ South Central or Southwest states
    ☐ Mountain states
    ☐ West Coast, north
    ☐ West Coast, south
    ☐ Alaska or Hawaii
    ☐ other

Appendix F

Sample EEOC Complaint Form

Form Approved
Budget Bureau No 44 R0304

U.S. DEPARTMENT OF LABOR EMPLOYMENT STANDARDS ADMINISTRATION WAGE AND HOUR DIVISION	**EMPLOYMENT INFORMATION FORM**

This report is authorized by Section 11 of the Fair Labor Standards Act. While you are not required to respond, submission of this information is necessary for the Division to schedule any compliance action. Information received by this Office will be treated confidentially.

1. PERSON SUBMITTING INFORMATION

A. Name (Print first name, middle initial, and last name) Mr. Miss Mrs.	B. Date
	C. Telephone number: (Or No where you can be reached)

D. Address: (Number, Street, Apt. No.)

_____

(City, County, State, ZIP Code)

_____

E. Check one of these boxes

☐ Present employee of establishment ☐ Former employee of establishment ☐ Job Applicant ☐ Other_____
(Specify: relative, union, etc)

2. ESTABLISHMENT INFORMATION

A. Name of establishment	B. Telephone Number

C. Address of establishment: (Number, Street)

(City, County, State, ZIP Code)

D. Estimate number of employees	E. Does the firm have branches? ☐ Yes ☐ No ☐ Don't know If "Yes", name one or two locations: _____

F. Nature of establishment's business: (For example; school, farm, hospital, hotel, restaurant, shoe store, wholesale drugs, manufactures stoves, coal mine, construction, trucking, etc.)

_____

G. If the establishment has a Federal Government or federally assisted contract, check the appropriate box(es).

☐ Furnishes goods ☐ Furnishes services ☐ Performs construction

H. Does establishment ship goods to or receive goods from other States?
☐ Yes ☐ No ☐ Don't know

3. EMPLOYMENT INFORMATION
(Complete A, B, C, D, E, & F if present or former employee of establishment; otherwise complete F only)

A. Period employed (month, year) From: _____ To: _____ (If still there, state present)	B. Date of birth if under 19 or if information concerns age discrimination Month _____ Day _____ Year _____

C. Give your job title and describe briefly the kind of work you do

_____

_____

Form WH-3 (Rev. Apr. 197

Afterword
Update to the New Edition

Today sexual harassment at the workplace is a well publicized and frequently discussed issue. This has not always been true. In recent years, many people have become aware of sexual harassment in the context of violence against women, others as a worker's issue, and others still as a management problem. Regardless of the focus, sexual harassment at the workplace has been recognized as a social problem that needs to be addressed and solved.

Sexual harassment was first addressed publicly by Working Women United Institute (WWUI) in Ithica, New York. Having conducted a preliminary survey of women workers and thus firmly convinced that sexual harassment was a serious problem, WWUI moved to New York City. They planned to address sexual harassment as one of many issues facing women workers. Soon afterwards, in 1976, the Alliance Against Sexual Coercion (AASC) was formed to focus exclusively on sexual harassment and to offer comprehensive services to individuals, and education and training to organizations and workplaces.

AASC had its roots in the anti-rape movement. Three women, all of whom had previously worked in rape crisis centers, started the organization in order to deal with the increasing number of calls that they received from women who were sexually assaulted at the workplace. They realized that the economic factor introduced in these cases made the usual rape crisis intervention insufficient. These women surveyed rape crisis centers around the country and found that sexual harassment calls and reports of rape at the workplace were frequent. Knowing that these women's centers and rape crisis centers were already overworked, the founding AASC members decided to set up separate services specifically for sexual harassment.

One of the first major events in our short history of sexual harassment was a 1976 survey conducted by Redbook magazine. In this self-reporting survey, 88% of the 9,000 respondents said that they received unwanted sexual attention on the job. In November 1977, Ms. magazine's cover story was about sexual harassment and several pieces on the topic were included in that issue. The response from feminists and working women was great. Shortly after the magazine was on the newsstands, Ms. and WWUI co-sponsored a speak-out on sexual harassment. Many women began to call WWUI and AASC to talk about their experiences of being harassed. Most of these clients had been harassed in the past or had quit their jobs because of harassment. Nevertheless, women still did not feel that they could speak publicly about their experience or seek support in their workplaces as public awareness was virtually non-existant.

During the next few years, AASC and WWUI worked to raise the issue to the public's attention through TV coverage, magazine and newspaper articles, and through national distribution of materials. During this period, three important books were released about sexual harassment including *The Secret Oppression: Sexual Harassment of Working Women* (Backhouse & Cohen), *Sexual Shakedown: The Sexual Harassment of Women on the Job* (Farley), and *Sexual Harassment of Working Women* (MacKinnon). Community and workplace educational workshops were given on a regular basis to introduce people to the issue and to sensitize them.

For the most part, there was very little labor union support or interest in sexual harassment. Unions worried that the issue might split the workforce and also did not take the concerns of women workers very seriously in general. Personnel and management did very little except trivialize the complaints of those women who did come forward. Thus, there were few options in the workplace and no outlets for the many women who needed to deal with the emotional aspects of being harassed.

The first major public coverage of sexual harassment began with hearings held in Washington, D.C. by the House of Representatives. Many individuals testified, including Diane Williams, a woman who was harassed in the Department of Justice and had filed a complaint; a member of the Women's Legal Defense Fund; and a representative from New Responses, a women's resource center in Washington, D.C. These women spoke about the issue, its emotional and economic effects on individuals, and its ramifications for all women workers. These hearings were part of a Congressional subcommittee's investigation of sexual harassment in the Federal government. The subcommittee instructed three departments to assume specific responsibilities with regard to sexual harassment. First, the Office of Personnel Management (OPM) issued a Policy Statement and Definition on Sexual Harassment and instructed other departments and independent agencies in the Federal government to develop policy statements and grievance procedures to regulate sexual harassment. OPM was also to initiate training for Federal workers. Secondly, the subcommittee requested that the Meris Systems Protection Board (MSPB) conduct a comprehensive survey on sexual harassment in the Federal government. A cross-section of male and female employees was sampled to provide quantitative (the magnitude of the problem) and qualitative (descriptions of incidents, attitudes about workplace behaviors) information. The third request was of the Equal Employment Opportunity Commission (EEOC) to improve the processing of sexual harrassment complaints, including training EEOC officials in responding sensitively to these reports.

What does it mean that the Federal government legitimized the issue that feminists had previously been trying to call attention to for three years? There are several positive results of this involvement and interest with sexual harassment.

First, as stated, the legitimization of the issue. Sexual harassment in the workplace is now seen as a problem for women workers that needs attention. This is particularly helpful in pressuring private sector companies to acknowledge sexual harassment. If the Federal government addresses the topic, then private businesses have to take notice as well. Secondly, public awareness meant the beginning of Federally funded training sessions to sensitize people in the workplace about sexual coercion. This had been the wish of all groups working on the issue since the beginning and finally access to employees at their work site on worktime was possible.

There are, however, certain problems created by the Federal government's key role in defining sexual harassment. The government does not share a feminist perspective and analysis of the problem. It is primarily concerned with management and personnel solutions rather than union or rank and file remedies. Consequently there are certain provisions lacking in remedies created by the Federal government. For example, it is not possible for workers or their advocates to monitor the procedures or to check for retaliatory behavior from the harasser when a woman complains. Also, the government does not require certain provisions in its policies that are crucial to us as feminists. These include some kind of direct services or counseling for women being harassed, and strict confidentiality of complaints. While all EEOC cases are handled confidentially, specific guidelines on sexual harassment should recognize the feelings of shame, fear and powerlessness that inhibit women from reporting. Although AASC is very glad to see sexual harassment legitimized and recognized as a social problem, we now face the problem of evaluating solutions posed by the Federal sector. Ironically, it has now become harder to pose alternative ideas or solutions to the problem of sexual harassment.

The issuing of guidelines by EEOC in April, 1980 is the most important event to date in the history of sexual harassment. These new guidelines define sexual harassment clearly as a form of sex discrimination. This understanding of sexual harassment had been previously established in the courts, but now women can file complaints of sexual harassment with their local Human Rights Commissions and with the EEOC since sexual harassment is in direct violation of these guidelines.

The EEOC guidelines have three major components: 1) Defining sexual harassment, 2) Clarifying who is responsible, and 3) Requiring preventative measures to be taken. Each of these elements is paraphrased below from the final amendment to guidelines on sexual harassment, issued in November, 1980.

Sexual harassment is defined as unwelcome sexual advances, requests for sexual favors, and other verbal or physical conduct of a sexual nature when submission to such conduct is made either explicitly or implicitly a term or condition of an individual's employment. Responsibility for sexual harassment is given to an employer, employment agency, or joint apprenticeship committee or labor organization. These entities are then responsible for their acts and those of their agents and supervisory employees with respect to sexual harassment regardless of whether the specific acts complained of were authorized or even forbidden by the employer.

Prevention is noted to be the best tool for the elimination of sexual harassment. An employer is required to take all steps necessary to prevent sexual harassment from occuring, such as affirmatively raising the subject, expressing strong disapproval, developing appropriate sanctions, informing employees of their rights under the EEOC guidelines to contest sexual harassment, and developing methods to sensitize all concerned.*

Once the guidelines were issued, AASC was flooded by requests from individuals wanting information about the problem, advice on how to set up policy statements and grievance procedures, and trainings for EEO officers. The demand had steadily grown, but it increased dramatically with the issuance of the EEOC guidelines. There have been certain shifts that we have noted. We no longer have to search for publicity. We now receive numerous requests from TV, magazines, newspapers, and radio for materials. This is certainly a major change from the mid-70's. There have also been changes in who requests information from us. Before April, most of our mail and phone calls were from clients, feminist activists, or social change oriented groups. We now receive a lot of our mail from management wanting information on effective personnel policies, and from consulting firms who want to do trainings for management about sexual harassment. Also, because state Human Rights Commissions and EEOC now process sexual harassment complaints, we receive many requests for information and training from EEO officers in the public sector.

We see a shift in emphasis from women who are being harassed to individuals in management, regulatory and policy-making agencies. The EEOC guidelines give an appearance and reassurance that adequate solutions for sexual harassment now exist. In most cases, this reassurance is false. The EEOC guidelines are definitely important, but the question of implementation within the workplace still remains. No mechanisms exist to monitor policy statements or grievance procedures, and there is no means to check the effectiveness of those procedures that do exist. There is an additional problem because complicated and detailed procedures make women less willing to file a complaint and feel uncomfortable because the atmosphere is so hostile. A law or regulation has never

---

*It should be noted that the future of sexual harassment legislation and training efforts is unclear under the Reagan administration. Reagan's Transition Team has recommended a complete freeze on all EEOC suits for one year. In addition, they feel it is impossible to eliminate sexual harassment, and that the EEOC guidelines have led to a "barrage of trivial complaints against employers."

been enough to fight discrimination although it does give others addressing the issue a strong base to stand on.

In conclusion, we want to refocus attention on the groups other than the Federal government who are working on sexual harassment. The government alone has not brought this problem before the public, defined it, and acted to remedy it. Over the last five years, many women's centers and rape crisis centers have provided sexual harassment services and numerous independent groups have been formed to deal exclusively with sexual harassment.

Management is now interested in sexual harassment because of the new EEOC guidelines, but employment associations and unions have also become concerned. Sexual harassment clauses are being added to union contracts, grievance procedures are being changed, and general worker education about sexual harassment and sexism is advocated by unions as preventative measures. Sexual harassment is no longer seen as an issue that will split the workforce, but as a serious working women's issue. Union women's committees and Health and Safety committees have begun to examine the problem and view it as an occupational hazard that needs to be changed. This support from labor represents an important shift in the possibilities for minimizing and eliminating sexual harassment. Union support as well as outside resource groups for both unionized and non-unionized women are important to provide places where women can talk about the harassment and strategize about their options.

The emphasis of these labor and women's groups, in contrast to management and consulting firms', is on the fact that concern about sexual harassment stems from broader issues of women's safety, sexism, and power relations in the workplace. These issues provide an important context for working on sexual harassment. Unfortunately, labor and women's groups have to compete with management consulting firms for the opportunity to train and sensitize people about the issue from different perspectives.

In summary, we find government and industry's recent interest in sexual harassment is at first glance somewhat puzzling. It can be viewed as their economic interest and our political interest fortunately coinciding. For years, sexual harassment of working women was ignored or laughed about. Suddenly within a year's time, we find a significant focus on this issue from all sectors of public and private management. In the second section of our Update, we discuss some of the reasons for this upsurge in interest by management as well as some of the problematic aspects of the recent legal and bureaucratic options developed to solve the problem.

PART TWO: SEXUAL HARASSMENT TODAY: AN ANALYSIS

Why Management Cares

Any issue acknowledged as a "problem" by employers requires time and money to "solve" it, and generally employers do not spend money on employees unless they have to. Let's examine some possible explanations about why management cares.

The Federal law that provides the basis for sex discrimination is Title VII of the 1964 Civil Rights Act. Title VII is the section of the act that prohibits discrimination on the basis of race, sex or other specific factors in employment. The EEOC is the regulatory agency created by Title VII to enforce the law. The recent EEOC guidelines mentioned earlier were developed to specifically address sexual harassment under Title VII.

All employers, including Federal, state, and local government agencies, and organizations and companies with more than 15 employees, could face potential suit for permitting the sexual harassment of their workers. Sexual harassment is defined as a form of sex discrimination and such suits can be costly and time consuming. Courts have awarded women sizable amounts of back pay and damages to compensate them for being sexually harassed. Management is obviously anxious to avoid these suits, which bring adverse publicity as well. If a company is found to practice sex discrimination, chances are that it is also not complying with mandatory affirmative action policies. The Office of Federal Contract Compliance monitors companies with Federal contracts and can withdraw funds on the basis of discrimination or lack of commitment to affirmative action. This is another example of how sexual harassment can cost big money to employers.

A second reason why employers are concerned with sexual harassment is productivity. Management, especially those with "efficiency" consultants understands that sexual harassment reduces the productivity of women workers. Any situation that creates non-productive stress reduces the work output. Stress results in absenteeism, increased work-place accidents, reduced concentration on specific tasks, and uncontrolled high turnover. For these reasons, employers are willing to try to reduce sexual harassment.

Sexual harassment, viewed as an occupational hazard, has great potential as a rallying point for organizing women workers. Our experience at the Alliance is that women who come together and discuss their experiences with sexual harassment almost universally identify with each others' anecdotes and begin to recognize the similarity in their plight. These sorts of alliances and connections between women provide tremendous incentive for beginning a women's committee, employee association, or concerted activity group. These types of worker groups are very threatening to most employers. It is much safer, from management's perspective, to take control of sexual harassment into their own hands rather than find themselves with a strongly organized union.

All three of these reasons (law suits, decreased productivity, and potential organizing) imply that it is in the interest of employers to comply with Federal guidelines, develop internal personnel policies, and initiate their own mechanisms to control sexual harassment. As activist organizations and progressive individuals working on this issue, we must keep clear about why management cares. The understanding of sexual harassment's root causes as well as the types of solutions management offers are sure to be different than those put forward by women workers or their advocates. We have to continue to discuss sexual harassment in the context of its origins in a sexist society, and a society with a rigid workplace hierarchy, and not settle for policies and procedures that aim to protect management from "trouble". Let's now look at the remedies offered to working women through personnel policies and Federal legislation.

Dangers of Legal and Bureaucratic Solutions for Sexual Harassment

With detailed Federal guidelines, enforcement agencies, and an increasing body of case law, we now have a veritable sexual harassment bureaucracy. We are all aware of the frustrations and inefficiencies of bureaucracies. Although we feel encouraged by the fact that women now have someplace to file sexual harassment complaints, we are also concerned about certain elements of these bureaucratic solutions.

Bureaucratic and legalistic solutions concentrate on the individual case rather than group action. Instead of focusing on general behavior and power dynamics, legal processes deal with "who did what to whom". People then perceive sexual harassment in terms of individual cases rather than as more general social behavior. This isolates individual women and perpetuates the common notion that sexual harassment is a personal problem rather than a social one.

Second, when one brings a sexual harassment complaint through a legal bureaucracy, one is forced to focus on the procedure rather than the harassment. Well-meaning, but overworked people, have to codify and reduce the situation into narrowly defined terms to fit the complaint to the regulations and to keep pace with their workload.

This type of process is not ideal for handling complaints of any kind, and it is particularly problematic for sexual harassment. Being sexually harassed is a very distressing, frightening, and insulting experience that makes most women feel very angry, guilty, powerless, or generally emotional. Bureaucracies and the workers that administer them are in no way equipped to acknowledge or respond to this range of feelings. The reality of what it means to be sexually harassed on the job is quickly lost in the procedural mess.

There are certain problems women encounter in dealing with bureaucracies specifically because of their situation as women. The frequent situation of women as workers *and* home-keepers makes these bureaucratic solutions even more difficult. Women with a double-day have little time and energy for the lengthy procedures of filing papers, affidavits, finding witnesses, etc. An additional problem some women face is that of being unequipped to stand up to the lengthy process because of timidity and lack of assertiveness in the face of more powerful opposition or even benign neglect. Success in a bureaucratic maze depends upon an unusually large degree of persistence and self-confidence.

A third problem that women of color face is the subtle and not so subtle racism that is woven throughout the legal/bureaucratic system. It takes certain kinds of skills, unconscious in people of privileged background, to manipulate bureaucracies in your favor. Statistically, women of color are subjected to more sexual harassment than white women, and face worse recriminations should they complain about the harassment. For Third World women, it is hard to sort out sexual harassment from racial harassment. This confusion makes it even harder to pursue a legal channel which requires a narrow and "accurate" definition of the problem.

Finally, legal and bureaucratic solutions are economically discriminatory. In almost every bureaucratic grievance option, you are better off with a lawyer. Although technically many things can be done without a lawyer, it is still true that lawyers are best equipped to deal with the language and formalities involved in these processes. Thus, although these solutions are important and necessary, they are not feasible for all women who experience sexual harassment.

In addition to these problems posed by the new remedies for sexual harassment, we have seen another type of problem crop up during the past few years. Several successful legal and institutional cases, particularly in the university setting, have been against black harassers. It is not difficult to see that the legal system works most effectively against defendants who are the most vulnerable. In these cases, it has been black men. Racism thus affects public perceptions of the nature of sexual harassment and undermines the process of dealing with the real problems for women workers. Our concern with sexual harassment is connected to our concerns with other forms of sexism, racism, and oppression in society. We need to guard against situations in which sexual harassment is used as a tool to further perpetuate the racism in our midst.

In the same manner that black men have been targeted as harassers more often than white men, we have seen sexual harassment charges aimed at other more "vulnerable" men. Union organizers, political activists, out-spoken critics, and gay people have been the recipients of these allegations. In the military, with studies showing very high levels of heterosexual harassment, a disproportionate number of charges have been brought against women for harassing other women or men for harassing other men.

The media's role in bringing certain cases to public attention should also be noted. All of these examples of relatively vulnerable people being reprimanded for sexual harassment are statistically exceptional cases. Survey results and AASC's caseload indicate that sexual harassment is widespread, and predominantly intraracial and male-to-female in occurence. However, the typical case of a white male executive or professional harassing a white female co-worker or subordinate seems not to be considered newsworthy.

Again, we have to be clear about the differences between why we as feminists and workers are concerned with sexual harassment, and why management is concerned. We do not want sexual harassment to become a way to divide people rather than a problem that working people of all kinds can join together to eliminate. We have to make certain that the remedies and options we choose cannot be manipulated in ways that are unfair and oppressive to other people who are also vulnerable.

The sources of sexual harassment stem from pervasive sexism in our society and sexist attitudes toward women as people and as workers. We cannot legislate and regulate men's views about women in our society, nor can we legislate cooperation amongst members of different strata of the workforce when their interests conflict.

Many people believe that, "a woman's place is in the home." Often, employers and co-workers do not take women seriously as full time steady workers. The assumption is that: she works to keep herself busy, not to support herself and possibly her children. The facts are just the opposite. Seven out of ten women work. Sexual harassment comes out of this lack of respect for women as workers, it's a way of saying, "you don't belong here."

Women are seen as sexual objects rather than as independent actors in the world. One example of this is the "physical qualities" many women are forced to rely on in job-hunting. Waitresses, receptionists, secretaries, stewardesses, and countless others are all *required* to meet certain traditionally defined standards of beauty. Women in other jobs still face the dilemma of "pleasing" the male job interviewer with an attractive appearance.

Despite the fact that more than 50% of women work, male dominance is still the reality in the workplace and sexual harassment serves as a constant reminder. Harassment of women on the job is not only accepted, but is at times expected. Sexual banter is often the standard form of communication between men and women, but such banter takes on a new dimension on the job. It becomes very difficult for a woman to speak out against unwanted sexual attention from her supervisor when she must then face the retaliation and reprisals that will most likely follow.

Women are concentrated in low-paying, dead-end jobs. A multitude of reasons explain this, but the fact remains that workers at the bottom of the labor force hierarchy have the least power and the fewest options to defend themselves. Women, and particularly Third World women, are especially susceptible to harassment because of their vulnerability as women in a sexist workplace and as severely exploited workers. The difficulties women face in resisting harassment largely relate to their insecure and unprotected position as workers.

At the same time, sexual harassment undermines women's job performance by causing dissatisfaction and fear, which often results in high rates of absenteeism and turnover. Poor job performance simply reinforces the low status of women workers and complicates the over-all picture of women workers gaining some power and control. So we witness a circular process whereby the low status of women as people and as workers legitimates harassment and then the harassment itself serves to maintain that status.

This situation does not imply that male workers have it great and really stand to benefit from harassing their female co-workers. Work is competitive and insecure — many men fear the threat of losing jobs to women. This is particularly true of the occupations that have been entirely male in the past. Again, these men do not accept women as co-workers with the same need to work as their own. Sexual harassment is ultimately a way of saying, "get out of my job." It is an expression of power and hostility that is sexual in nature.

If we step back and look at the situation of workers in general, it is clear that male workers do not reap large benefits from harassing their female counterparts. Sexual harassment, through helping to keep women workers in low-paying, dead-end jobs, serves as part of a complex of sex-discrimination that women face on the job. Discrimination means, in real terms, that women take home 59¢ for every $1.00 earned by a man, that women are more easily hired and fired than men, and essentially more easily exploited. If women serve as a cheap and expendable labor force, the bargaining power and strength of male workers is threatened.

What we realize as we trace the origins of sexual harassment is that this issue is not a singular problem that women face on the job. It is connected to the other dilemmas working women encounter such as equal pay, promotions, steady work, and general respect. It is part of women's attempts to be viewed as steady, full-time workers.

Sexual harassment, and sex discrimination in general, manifest the larger problems of sexism in our society. We must keep this relationship in mind when we think about our goals and strategies for eliminating sexual harassment.

Our primary goal is to challenge the root cause of sexual harassment — sexism. We want to think about sexual harassment in a context that connects it to other problems women face so that women fighting against sexual harassment are also taking positive steps toward gaining more control over other aspects of their lives.

An important feature of a strategy directed at challenging sexism is that women are *active* participants. Such strategies place a priority on the *process* of women learning to join together and speak out against the exploitive aspects of their lives. Through acting and talking together, women can begin to view sexual harassment as a *problem* to counter rather than a *condition* of work that women simply have to accept.

In keeping with these goals of challenging sexism and empowering women, our strategy at AASC is to explore the relationships that exist between women at a given workplace. We encourage women to seek support from their female co-workers to take some sort of direct action to stop the harassment. That action could be anything from sending the harasser an anonymous note to confronting the harasser en masse with other women. Whatever the action, the fact is that the woman being harassed takes the situation into her own hands and makes choices about her tactics. She has not given up control of the situation to an outside investigator or agency. We realize, of course, that certain harassment situations do *not* fit this type of model. These are only guidelines to keep in mind.

In conclusion, AASC recognizes that legal and procedural strategies are necessary and important, but they narrow the scope of the issue, rather than broaden it. We must make certain that they exist along side other strategies that focus on education and organization of women to take power in their homes and their jobs. Again, we must also realize that there are many different categories of working women. An over-all strategy that we use should be accessible to all women. Women have different resources available to them, thus certain options are more likely for some women than others. A single working mother with three children will not find a long, costly legal suit as appealing an option as a single woman without financial obligations. We need to make the whole spectrum of options available so that a woman can choose the course of action that best fits with her life situation. Our biggest concern is that the future of sexual harassment not become a future of complaint procedures and legislative change that makes no effort to seriously include strategies that make sense to a range of women.

Sexual harassment will never go away until women begin to take control over their lives both inside and outside the workplace. This vision helps us to conceive of a variety of long-term strategies for women along side the more clear-cut legal alternatives. We must keep this perspective in mind as we assess our work and formulate new ways of fighting sexual harassment that speak to the needs of *all* women.

Suggested Further Reading

Backhouse, Constance and Leah Cohen, *The Secret Oppression: Sexual Harassment of Working Women.* Toronto: Macmillan of Canada, 1979.

Farley, Lin, *Sexual Shakedown.* New York: McGraw-Hill, 1978.

MacKinnon, Catherine A., *Sexual Harassment of Working Women: A Case of Sex Discrimination.* New Haven: Yale University Press, 1979.

"A Proposal: We Need Taboos on Sex at Work." *Redbook,* April 1978, p. 31.

"A Shocking Look at What Men Do to Women on the Job." *Redbook,* November 1976.

"Sexual Harassment at the Workplace: Historical Notes." *Radical America,* July-August 1978, Vol. 12, No. 4, p. 25.

"Sexual Harassment on the Job: How to Spot It and How to Stop It." *Ms.,* November 1977, p. 47.

"Sexual Harassment: How You Can Fight Off Your Boss." *Mother Jones,* June 1978.

"Sexual Pressure on the Job." *McCalls,* March 1978, p. 43.

"The Working Woman: Sexual Harassment." *Ladies Home Journal,* June 1977, p. 24.

Aegis — Magazine on Ending Violence Against Women. AASC does a regular column generally dealing with issues of sexual harassment. Subscriptions may be obtained by sending to:

FAAR
Box 21033
Washington, DC 20009
Rates: Individual — one year (6 issues) $ 8.75
      Institutions $20.00

The Alliance Against Sexual Coercion and Working Women United Institute are in the process of compiling a comprehensive bibliography on sexual harassment which should be completed in the late fall. Inquiries should be mailed to AASC.

MATERIALS YOU CAN ORDER
from
Alliance Against Sexual Coercion
P.O. Box 1, Cambridge, Mass. 02139
(617) 482-0329

Mitos Y Realidads Sobre El Hostigamiento Sexual $1.00 per copy
A short paper on the myths and facts about sexual harassment is now available in Spanish translation. Other selected materials will be published soon.

Sexual Harassment: An Annotated Bibliography $7.00 per copy
This 30-page-booklet will summarize the legal developments that apply to sexual harassment. This includes a review of statutory law, regulatory guidelines, and major legal precedents. Some of the subjects covered are: civil law, Title VII (sex discrimination) information, unemployment rights, worker compensation information, and the legal rights of students under Title IX. Lawyers, law students, and anyone considering legal action will find that this guide organizes information in an efficient and useful manner.

Combatiendo El Hostigamiento Sexual $2.50 per copy
Traduccion de algunos capitulos del manual de abogacia en ingles. La información incluye Opciones Legales, Definicion del Hostigamiento Sexual, Mitos y Realidades acerca del Hostigamiento, y Consejeria para Agencias de Servicios Sociales.

Why Men Harass (Men Who Harass) $2.00 per copy
Interviews with men about sexual harassment compiled by AASC in an effort to explore the motivations behind harassment. Interviewees include men who are working against harassment as well as men who harass. This article provides important insights into a male perspective on sexual harassment.

University Grievance Procedures, Title IX, and Sexual Harassment
$4.00 per copy
A 30 page pamphlet discussing legal and extra-legal options for harassed students. It contains clear, concise explanations of Title IX and its application in universities, general information on grievance procedures, and specifics on how to develop sensitive and workable grivance procedures. Essential for all working in education.

Sexual Harassment at the Workplace: Historical Notes, by Mary Bularzik
$2.00 per copy
Originally published in *Radical America*, this article is the first and only historical treatment of sexual harassment. Well-written and powerfully documented through the use of journals and personal histories.

To order: Shipments of the materials listed above are made when the order is prepaid or includes an organization purchase order. All prices include bookrate or third class postage. Additional charge for first class postage, please specify. Make checks payable to A.A.S.C., PO Box 1, Cambridge, MA 02139.

Do not combine your order for these materials with your order for the books listed on the next two pages.

Other books you can order from
ALYSON PUBLICATIONS

Beyond the Fragments: $6.95
Feminism and the making of socialism
by Sheila Rowbotham, Lynne Segal and Hilary Wainwright
  Three women who have been active in both feminist and socialist politics examine the implications of the women's movement on leftist politics in this ground-breaking work. They argue not just for a rhetorical acceptance of feminism, but for a redefinition of priorities, a new approach to theory and consciousness, and for an open and searching examination of past and present forms of political organization. (Publication date: October 1981. Orders received earlier will be shipped immediately upon publication.)

The Men With the Pink Triangle $4.95
by Heinz Heger
  For decades, historians have ignored the persecution of homosexuals by the Nazi regime. Now a man who survived six years in the Nazi concentration camps has finally told about that terrible era. **The Men With the Pink Triangle** is the intensely personal story of a young Austrian student who was abruptly arrested by the Gestapo in 1939 for being homosexual. He spent the next six years in German concentration camps; like other homosexual prisoners, he was forced to wear a pink triangle on his shirt so he could be readily identified for special mistreatment. His story is often depressing, but it is one you will never forget. 'One of the Ten Best Books of the Year' (Richard Hall, *The Advocate*).

Energy, Jobs and the Economy $3.45
by Richard Grossman and Gail Daneker
  Sure you're in favor of solar energy. But what about your Uncle Joe, who's worried that without nuclear power we'll have blackouts and plant closings and that he may lose his job? This highly readable book shows that solar and renewable energy sources are not only safer than nuclear power, they're also better for the economy and for working people.

The Incredible Shrinking American Dream $6.95
by Estelle Carol, Rhoda Grossman and Bob Simpson
  History should have been this much fun in high school! The authors have written a comic-book history of the US that will entertain you while it brings to light the often-forgotten history of working people, women and minorities. 'Terrific! A solid class analysis of the American past, in words and pictures that are a delight to the eye and to the funny bone' (Bertell Ollman, creator of the *Class Struggle* game).

Reflections of a Rock Lobster: $4.95
A story about growing up gay
by Aaron Fricke

Guess who's coming to the prom! No one in Cumberland, Rhode Island, was surprised when Aaron Fricke appeared at his high school prom with a male date. He had sued his school for the right to do so, and the media had been full of the news.

Yet for the first sixteen years of his life, Fricke had closely guarded the secret of his homosexuality. *Reflections of a Rock Lobster* is his story about growing up with this secret. With insight and humor, Fricke tells how he first became aware of his homosexual feelings in childhood, then learned to hide them from adults, and then to repress his feelings completely, before he finally developed a positive gay identity. '*Rock Lobster* is simply the most realistic, revealing, painful, insightful and — finally — joyful story about growing up gay in America that you will ever read.' (John Preston in *New York Native*.)

Young, Gay and Proud $2.95

One high school student in ten is gay. Here is the first book ever to address the problems and needs of that often-invisible minority, helping young people deal with questions like: Am I really gay? What would my friends think if I told them? Should I tell my parents? Does anybody else feel the way I do?

Health Care for the People: Studies from Vietnam $6.95
by Dr. Joan McMichael

This account of medical services in Vietnam will inspire everyone who believes that a humane health system is indeed possible. Organized in the face of enormous adversity, the Vietnamese system puts to shame the medical establishments of many far more "developed" countries.

The Healing Art of Clara Walter $2.95
A new approach to health care
byClara Walter

At the age of thirty-nine, Clara Walter used natural cures to heal lifelong health problems and injuries that had been called incurable. The next fifty years of her life were devoted to developing these natural cures. Here, Walter explains her program, documenting the results she has achieved and showing the way for others to use her methods.

Ask for these titles in your bookstore. If unavailable locally, you may order them directly from Alyson Publications, Dept. B3, PO Box 2783, Boston, MA 02208. Please enclose full payment with your order and add 75¢ postage on orders for one book. (If you order two or more books, we'll pay postage.)